So you dream of being a
Chief Executive?

Julian

You know you don't want to be one of these ....

with every good wish

John April 2002

This book is dedicated to Alexander and Christopher Viney – two nascent business leaders?

So you dream of being a
Chief Executive?

The **Route** to the **Top**

JOHN VINEY

CAPSTONE

Copyright © 2002 by John Viney

The right of John Viney to be identified as the author of this work has been asserted in accordance with the Copyright, Designs and Patents Act 1988

First published 2002 by
Capstone Publishing Ltd (A John Wiley & Sons Co.)
8 Newtec Place
Magdalen Road
Oxford OX4 1RE
United Kingdom
http://www.capstoneideas.com

British Library Cataloguing in Publication Data

A CIP catalogue record for this book is available from the British Library

ISBN 1-84112-144-4

Typeset by
Forewords, 109 Oxford Road, Cowley, Oxford

Printed and bound by
T.J. International Ltd, Padstow, Cornwall

This book is printed on acid-free paper

Contents

Acknowledgements

I have now been writing business books for over a decade and have had to weave writing around my professional life as a business consultant. I do not have the luxury of blocks of time available to complete a book in a few long sittings. If you, the reader fail to identify the joins in the construction of this book, then this is entirely due to Judith Osborne who acts as an editor, writer, coach and counsel to me. To her I owe a great deal of thanks.

This book also owes a great deal to the business leaders I have met over the past twenty or more years. I wish to thank all of them and hope that they do not spot themselves too easily in the text . . .

Preface

So you dream of being a Chief Executive? In the course of my career as a search consultant, few people I have met would deny that this is their dream. I have spent long hours assessing would-be Chief Executives and have observed large numbers of CEOs operating at the helm of numerous businesses. I have, I suppose, an excellent vantage point from which to understand what it takes to be a CEO, and how best to get there. Perhaps it is an occupational hazard for all headhunters that the professional spills over into the private such that, outside work, even relatively chance acquaintances seem to want to know from me how they can position themselves to secure the top job at wherever it is they work. All the evidence points to the fact that a book which seeks to plot a course through the labyrinth of corporate life to the boardroom might be of some use and interest.

Specifically, then, this book is targeted – to use a current business phrase – at a clear number of groups:

- Senior business figures who are close to being considered as the next Chief Executives of their companies.
- Mid-career, high achievers who hope to be a Chief Executive at some time in their career – ideally as soon as possible.

- Budding business leaders of tomorrow now in their twenties to early thirties who want to understand the road to the top of business.
- University students and recent graduates starting out on their path to the top.

This book considers the talent, skills and experience necessary to be an effective Chief Executive, and does not neglect to consider those who might have these skills, but might not have found the right moment or environment. If offers options here too.

Where you start with this book is dictated to an important extent by where you are in your career. The more advanced your career, the later on you can start to dip into this book. The chapters are organized chronologically as follows:

Chapter 1 considers the decision to enter business in the first place. Is it really the right place for you? Do you understand what business is about? Are your values consistent with those of a corporation? The chapter considers the differences between corporate business people and entrepreneurs and between leaders and managers.

Chapter 2 looks at education. There is no right form of education for making it to the top and this chapter considers the very different ways in which education can be used to propel a career forward but also considers how it can hold some back, notably entrepreneurs. The chapter then moves on to look at the first career decisions, how they should be made and judged.

Chapter 3 ponders a question that has long concerned me, namely why so many people who are successful in their twenties suddenly disappear in their thirties. Some of this is down to a misapprehension of how business is organized and so the chapter considers closely attitudes to authority. It also looks at the fraught question of why women unquestionably hit a glass ceiling and offers strategies for avoidance.

Chapter 4 is about consolidation. The steps you will need to take to secure the Chief Executive role. We jump forward to look at the issues of concern to the Nominating Committee who will consider your fate in the future. Based on their requirements the chapter looks at the sort of experiences you need to accumulate, focusing on rounding out and working on weaknesses as well as strengths.

Chapter 5 goes on to look at the skills required by a Chief Executive and then recaps on the combination of skills and experience required to go from raw recruit to Chief Executive, spending time looking at the very important issues of mutual respect and trust.

Chapter Six considers what you might do if you have not been successful on the first attempt. For some it might be sensible to try again in another organization. Others might decide to settle for a major Board role as a colleague to the new Chief Executive. But there are also other options. This chapter shows that even if this dream has not been realized you can dream anew!

In a brief afterword we give the final word to the successful Chief Executive and consider what can ensure that having gained the role, he or she can maintain their success.

CHAPTER 1

Is business the right place for you?

What business is and is not. The rise of business and demise of other occupations. The values of business versus the public sector, the professions and the voluntary sector. The differences between corporate leaders, corporate managers and entrepreneurs. A value check. Do you fit?

So you dream of being a Chief Executive? Since you are reading this book there is a fair chance that you do indeed cherish a desire to run something, to be selected above your peers and entrusted with the future of an enterprise. It is a fair assumption that you are ambitious, reasonably competitive but perhaps a little bewildered as to how you can set about making the dream reality. A generation or so ago, an aspiring Chief Executive had limited control over his (and it usually was *his*) destiny. He would trust that the paternalist institution of which he was a part would offer him a series of challenging assignments such that he would be able to prove himself over and above his peers. In some twenty-five years he would be rewarded with a seat on the board and in due course the hotseat itself. It helped if he had been born into the

appropriate class, attended the appropriate educational establishments, held membership of the appropriate clubs and
played the appropriate games. Not infrequently, proving himself meant proving that he would manage the status quo and
avoid any unseemly rocking of boats. A quarter of a century
on, the world of business has become increasingly meritocratic
on the one hand and decreasingly paternalist on the other.
Playing safe is no longer the low-risk strategy it once was.
Innovation is valued and leadership is more fashionable
(though sadly no more evident) than in previous decades. One
has to make it to the top by dint of one's own record and on the
evidence of one's own abilities. In short, you, the aspiring, able
Chief Executive, hold your own destiny in your hands.

This is, of course, for those interested in the health and future
of our corporations, good news. However, the super-abundance
of opportunity is a mixed blessing for those who want to take
full advantage of it. There is no single route to the top. There is
no one elixir of success. In a diverse market where old econ-
omy meets new and values and judgements of excellence are
shifting daily it is easy for an aspiring executive to make a
wrong choice and find him- or herself in a career blind alley.
The route to the top is truly labyrinthine and sometimes it may
be a case of superior navigation skills that can determine one
person's success and another's failure. The object of this book
is to identify the key staging posts in a career, to identify the
watersheds and critical decision points. It distils the accumulated observation of the last couple of decades advising boards
on the appointments of Chief Executives. It is an insider's
view into the issues that dominate in the decision-making process but it also brings to bear observation of numerous

successful people, many of whom have pursued alternative routes to the top but made it there – and stayed there. This is a Rough Guide and a Michelin guide in one. It is intended to be dipped into by young and not so young, by those starting out and those in the middle of their career. There are even some words of hope for those who feel they have missed their moment. It is a book which will offer some answers but in the main will pose questions that will enable the would-be Chief Executive to assess whether the dream to be a Chief Executive is a pipe-dream or not.

Managing your personal brand

Today careers demand to be managed and an aspiring business leader must adopt a clear strategy for him or herself. Career management may be likened to brand management; you are your own brand and you can develop that brand, market it, adjust it to suit changing conditions; perhaps once in your career you may be called upon to reinvent yourself and conduct a subtle rebranding exercise. The important issue is to treat oneself as a premium brand and not as a commodity and to give thought to packaging, values, perception and markets. No marketeer would attempt to devise a new product without carefully considering the market onto which it will be launched. Rather, he or she would carefully analyse the market through hard data and close inspection of the competitors and their offerings and would proceed on the basis of finding a match. The first question the aspiring Chief Executive should consider, then, is which market is the appropriate one to allow him or her to realize that original dream. The concern of this chapter is principally with the choice of milieu or market. Is business the right place for you? The question may seem a facile one, but an understanding of the values and concerns at the heart of business is fundamental. If those values and concerns prove, ultimately, anathema to you, then no matter how talented you are you will not succeed. Given that the Chief Executive must embody the values and culture of an organization, it stands to reason that they must have a deep conviction that those values are appropriate.

Business – destination of choice, or last resort?

Many people drift into business. They leave school or university a little uncertain of what to do and take on a job in a company in the spirit of buying time while they discover, by some magical process, what it is they really want to do. This can be true of the most driven and ambitious individual as much as for the undirected person with few aspirations and is, to some extent, the consequence of apparently diminishing choices. Previous generations had other options as they started to make their way in the world. For many men and women a career in the armed forces conferred rank and status, and offered opportunities to travel, acquire new skills and experience extraordinary events. While the military continues to offer these for some people it is fair to say that much of the status has been eroded and, happily, so have some of the opportunities: in a period of extraordinarily sustained peace on a world scale the notion of the armed forces remains rather out of fashion, September 11th, 2001 notwithstanding.

The professions have long offered status, security, reasonable wealth and intellectual stimulus. They have also often provided a congenial environment of collegiality and support. Most have been partnerships where a spirit of mutual support sustained the culture. In recent years new barriers to entry have been erected by professional bodies, keen to protect their reputation for excellence. Principal among these has been the move to make entry open only to graduates. No longer can a school leaver join a firm at sixteen and work through clerical grades before becoming articled. If the late developer wishes to train they will be required to study for a full degree and apply for entry as a graduate. In short, those seeking a professional career must come to that realization sufficiently early to ensure they gain a degree. The professions have changed substantially in their style of operation. While many remain partnerships, the style of those partnerships has altered. Younger, high-performing partners, often from homes much less wealthy than their older partner colleagues, have become reluctant to support those who have gone beyond their peak of performance. Old salary structures which once rewarded longevity (the much maligned 'points' lockstep system) have given way to performance-related rewards. In some sectors partnerships have been dissolved and companies have been incorporated in their wake. In short the professions have ceased to seem a rather cosy and comfortable way of life but are much like the very businesses they serve, intolerant of less than excellent performance.

There are, of course, other professional activities, such as teaching and medicine. In both cases, however, we have seen a marked erosion of status and a corresponding growth in workload. Schoolteachers are the subject of very careful scrutiny by regulators and by parents who are markedly more empowered than were their own parents. Today as parents we are consumers of an educational service supplied by teachers and schools, and where we experience disappointment in the quality of that service we make our displeasure known. The huge expansion of tertiary education has led to a proliferation of university teachers and, as in any market where there is a surplus, their value has fallen. This can be measured in the sharp decline of salary levels in real terms. No more can a professor expect to earn the equivalent of a top civil servant or a doctor. The state, quite simply, cannot support huge salary bills. Again, the universities are subject to careful regulation, just like schools, and here the consumers of the service are the students themselves who are now paying personally to receive the service. While doctors fare better in terms of remuneration they are experiencing a sharp decline in their status. Levels of trust have fallen sharply in the wake of a handful of highly publicized scandals and a general dissatisfaction with the perceived arrogance of many in the medical profession towards their patients.

I could continue with this litany of change since a shift towards business is one aspect of a shift in society. The concept of public service is as unfashionable as that of armed service. Trade unions have largely lost their power, and politics, while still a magnet for some, offers a future of constant uncertainty. The voluntary sector offers opportunity and is increasingly becoming more efficient and so more effective. Nevertheless the sector remains dogged by low pay and many processes and procedures which can be off-putting. Sport and music appeal strongly to the young and can give some genuine opportunity to young people and have successfully empowered young black adults in particular. Real success, however, comes to only a handful of people and the choice of either can lead to more heartache than happiness. Small wonder, in the light of the above, that business seems the only available option for many when they start out.

Business: good place or bad place?

To those on the outside business offers the chance to earn money, to attain a high standard of living and the comfort of clear structures which lend a sense of possibility and progression. Many people in business gain the opportunity to travel and, of course, there is always the sense that by managing others one can gain power. This alone can give business a sense of glamour and of purpose. But business is still, for many, a rather shadowy world. The British attitude to business can best be described as ambivalent. It is unquestionably the case that perceptions of business are changing but there remains a deep distrust. Indeed, this distrust is by no means confined to the UK. We only have to look at the growing international protest movement which takes as its focal point the role of the global organization to see that business is understood by some people to be something quite monstrous. In the post cold-war period the corporation is taking over as the new unknown and it is telling, perhaps, that the novelist most associated with cold-war espionage novels, John Le Carré, has in his recent novel *The Constant Gardener* turned his attention to a corporate threat. It is seldom the case that business matters move from the business pages (somewhere towards the back of newspapers) to the front page for anything but a negative report. Business heroism is never the subject of headlines and most people would be hard pushed to name many business heroes or might be more likely to know of them for their achievements outside business than from within. More people would know of Lord McLaurin because of his involvement in cricket or Archie Norman because of his political prominence in recent years than as the former Chief Executives of two of our most successful retailers. The tide is turning in business's favour. Greg Dyke, Director General of the BBC, has recognized the place of business in public life by appointing a business correspondent. This apparently small decision is actually a significant shift in attitude and, already Geoff Randell has brought business issues to the headlines.

Much of the British unease with business has its roots in a long held distaste for 'trade'. In fact, the British have been very successful traders, originally trading within our empire and following its collapse, with our Commonwealth colleagues. For generations, however, land not trade mattered to the British ruling classes, even if the land was bought and sustained by trade. In the novels of Jane Austen landowners have to go and tend to their overseas plantations – but this is trade at a safe distance. Those who gained huge fortunes in the course of the industrialization of Britain (and thus on our own doorsteps) sought to ennoble themselves by buying vast estates and educated their children in the manner of aristocrats rather than encouraging a continuing interest in commerce. Land has long signified leisure and largesse, trade has unpleasant connotations of labour, muck and dirt. Such attitudes find their way into the collective consciousness. Only a tiny percentage of the British population are aristocrats but millions are involved, however tangentially, in some form of business. Nevertheless, the old suspicion of business has persisted and the iniquitious British class system has encouraged a slavish respect for old money over new. Business is something that can and does enable people to achieve wealth beyond the dreams of avarice but that money, until recently, has not led to immediate respect and reverence. By and large in the past the British people have been more comfortable with faded gentility than with the flashy *nouveau riche*. And this is by no means only a British phenomenon but one that is evident across Europe, and which I consider at some length in *The Culture Wars*. Teenagers reading this might find such a statement surprising since their own value system so little reflects this attitude.

New money, new values?

There is little doubt that such attitudes are changing. Posh and Becks, the new aristocracy, are unashamedly the recipients of new money, albeit they come from the twin worlds of sport and pop where we typically attach folk-hero status to our best performers. In short, they can get away with being very rich because they have earned our approval. The various indices of the most wealthy in our society testify to a growing fascination with how money is made and by whom and, of course, numerous business figures (largely entrepreneurs) feature in such lists. The dot-com explosion of the late 1990s and the creation of a number of paper millionaires gave a certain glamour to the get-rich-quick approach which the subsequent collapse of the market has not entirely undermined. As the nation has grown wealthy and become consumption-obsessed the pursuit of wealth has come to seem a more acceptable practice. Bright graduates, with a sophisticated sense of their market value, soon spot that they can gain higher salaries in business than they can in the civil service or the public sector. As business becomes, increasingly, the destination of choice for graduates it will grow in status. It is the case that business is an all-encompassing term and many of the brightest graduates are attracted by those business activities with a markedly 'professional' hue, such as banking or management consulting where starting salaries are high and selection procedures so exacting that acceptance confers a degree of élitism.

The ambivalence towards business persists all the same. The phrase 'fat cats' has passed into the English language to describe those who have made vast sums of money through business, and, by inference, without just cause. Originally the phrase was used for the beneficiaries of privatization. Overnight, directors of formerly state-owned entities became wealthy without necessarily having performed in a way as to deserve such marked elevation in their income. Today the term is used more generally to describe people on the boards of businesses who make large sums of money. Little concern is given to the fact that in many (if not all) cases directors have performed extremely well and in so doing have generated wealth for shareholders. There remains a somewhat mealy-mouthed attitude to money and a failure to accept that making money for shareholders is a valid occupation. Those who decry the huge profits made by organizations fail to consider the sums made by the state through the success of enterprise. Pension provision, beyond the state, also depends upon exemplary corporate performance since so many major shareholders in leading enterprises are the pension funds. These pension funds, in turn, have played a part in trying to ensure that corporations respect the requirement for good and transparent governance.

What business is about

In any discussion of business it is impossible to move far from the matter of money. Businesses exist to generate wealth. Those working within businesses must therefore be committed to making money. It is the gauge, the tally of how successful your business skills are, the equivalent of votes to politicians. It is not the sole criterion on which people in business are judged, but the ability to make money is an important point of differentiation. To be more specific, business is about making profit not just money. Many, many businesses just generate a turnover to provide a living. The key in business is to make profits and then to reinvest them. Don't spend the profits – plough them back into a good business which will grow. Compounding works! Generating profits and delivering value are the most important elements of a successful business. Of course there are numerous other issues that contribute to corporate wellbeing, but most are subsidiary to, or supportive of, the fundamental profit principle. Many of the values that we associate with business are there to ensure that structures are created and sustained that will allow corporations to maximize their profitability and to do so in perpetuity. Businesses do not exist in isolation but in a fierce set of interrelationships where there may be partnerships, a network of needs and, inevitably, substantial competition. Successful businesses are those that find better solutions for their customers or offer better products than do their competitors. Success is not about decrying the competition but it is about beating it. In corporate life there is no embarrassment about wanting to be the best and a will to win is valorized. The British obsession with the underdog finds no favour on the stock markets. It is the top dog the markets celebrate.

Some popular myths

All the same there is a common conception that business is a bully, that big businesses squeeze out small and that there is no sense of honour or reverence for fair play. The fate of the small cornershop being forced out of business by the out-of-town superstore is a commonplace example of perceived corporate bullying. Nor can it be denied that such things have happened, although the strategic objective of the large retailer will have been to meet growing consumer demand for a different way of shopping in response to changing demographics and not to send small traders into bankruptcy. Businesses are about markets and spotting changing trends in those markets and adapting to meet them. Business simply operates by the same principles as the natural world – natural selection. Those ventures that are flexible and adapt will survive. So in the last twenty-five years we have seen the growing phenomenon of the Asian shopkeeper who works long hours to provide local access to essential goods at unsociable hours. These enterprising and hard-working entrepreneurs have, in a number of cases, gone on to build substantial enterprises, respecting rather than resisting scale.

There are more sinister examples of corporate bullying. One of the rare breed of business heroes is James Dyson, the inventor of a new type of vacuum cleaner. The history of his attempts to market his inventions is redolent of the worst types of industrial espionage, but misconduct on the part of some enterprises should not be seen as an indicator of misconduct on the part of all. We have seen several high-profile cases of match fixing in sport. We do not, however, automatically generalize from the specific and assume that all sportsmen are innately corrupt although, like all good businessmen and women top sportsmen and women play to win. We make heroes of our sportsmen but less often of our business people and perhaps in making a hero of Dyson we are not celebrating his originality and business-building prowess so much as celebrating the lone figure fighting the corporate brutes? Businesses are increasingly the subject of regulation and nowhere is this more evident than in relation to competition. The European Commission and local governments work actively to ensure that competition is fair and that undue dominance on the part of major corporations is held in check so the notion of the rogue and ruthless corporate pirate (in theory at least) is less and less likely to occur.

Competition

Competition is central to business life and those who engage with business must compete internally as well as externally. A would-be Chief Executive will, effectively, have to see off other challengers. Inevitably there are always some executives who compete by undermining others, but the best and most confident should compete on their own merits, driven by their desire for continual self-improvement and a clear sense of identifying with the success of the enterprise of which they are a member. For a long period after the Second World War the British mentality baulked at the notion of self-improvement. The growth of the welfare state and the powerful and well-intentioned lobby to protect the underprivileged had the unlooked-for consequence of bringing into question the legitimacy of personal advancement. This was best exemplified by soaring tax rates which supported the welfare state, but in so doing stifled enterprise. The long years of Thatcherism reversed some of this but the fanatical obsession with enterprise which characterized the period somehow positioned individual wealth as something against the common good. The values (and experiences) of the 1980s and the spectre of boom and bust left business with a legacy of ill-will. Whatever the rights and wrongs of the case it is now true to conclude that those who do want to better themselves can come out into the sun and strive with a freer conscience than for some decades.

In assessing both external and internal competition executives must exercise judgement. The exercise of judgement is an integral element of every walk of life. The civil servant must make judgements on policy, doctors on symptoms and treatment, and teachers on matters of discipline and curriculum on a daily basis. In corporate life, unless we make the rather spurious claim that the delivery of shareholder value is an altruistic exercise, most judgement is exercised for broadly selfish reasons. I want my company to be the best in its markets so I will study what all other members of that market are doing in order to identify opportunities for improvement. Alternatively, I want to progress in this organization so I will assess my colleagues to see where they excel and where I might be weak so as to minimize my weaknesses and maximize my strengths. These objectives lie at the heart of any business endeavour. Judgement in business is exercised towards these ends with the ultimate objective of coming out on top. For some this impetus to succeed can seem overly driven and, indeed, harsh. Some may reject business for its apparent want of altruism and overt individualism. Sometimes, of course, the desire to win can lead to activities which have a negative effect on the world; there is widespread dismay at the sale of cigarettes to minors, particularly in underdeveloped countries where the practice seems most prevalent. Similarly, the development of a market in processed milk in the underdeveloped world which has undermined the practice of breast-feeding can be seen to be an action of dubious intent. Business is open to unethical practice as much as any activity but, again, it is all too easy to generalize from a few examples. In these more enlightened times when businesses are conscious of the requirement to meet ethical and environmental obligations, there is a general recognition that business is about winning – but not at the cost of integrity and moral probity.

Teamwork

Few executives who operate entirely for their own ends are ever enduringly successful. At the heart of any successful enterprise or executive is a strong team element. Businesses operate in conjunction with their suppliers for the benefit of their customers. The executive team at the top of a corporation blends a series of distinct areas of expertise to create a unified approach to the market. The would-be Chief Executive who makes a practice of undermining his or her fellows on the way up may find when the top is finally reached that the team has been lost along the way. An isolated Chief Executive without a team of able executives rarely sustains success for long. So, business requires people to compete but to do so as part of a team.

Business leadership and self-selection

The requirement to compete, to innovate, to move things forward also brings with it a requirement for tenacity, energy and a certain tolerance for risk. There is little certainty in business which is prey to the movement of the global markets. For those who want a relatively comfortable existence, business leadership is unlikely to prove a safe harbour. For countless people who do not crave to lead, however, business does offer some certainty and safety. Most corporations are organised along hierarchical lines with clearly demarcated positions. If we were to follow the fortunes of a highly able group of young graduates in a business we would doubtless find that the majority will find their plateau somewhere up the hierarchy, often quite a way before the top is reached. Business can offer rewards both financial and emotional at the mid-point either in interesting functional or small general management roles, and successful organizations depend upon the disinclination of all able young people to make the sacrifices required to occupy a position of true leadership. Much is said about the decline of the cradle to grave mentality and it is certainly true that few companies guarantee a job for life. Despite this uncertainty there remains much scope for transferring from one organization to another and finding an appropriate niche in the business world. Failure, or only partial success, in one environment does not inevitably mean failure or only partial success in all. This book, however, is not concerned with the rank and file in business; it is concerned with those who will lead, and for this small community the future holds substantial sacrifice.

Business must and will become an all-consuming passion. Of course most business leaders appear to lead perfectly normal lives. They will marry, have children and grandchildren and even take the occasional holiday. In my experience, however, few top corporate executives, or, indeed, entrepreneurs, take much time off, using the phrase in the most general sense. In studying business leaders as I have done over many years and as I did in some detail in my last book *Drive: Leadership in Business and Beyond*, I was struck by the obsessive interest most betrayed in business. Few have time to indulge in any passion for art, music or literature, and those who loved sport in their youth generally have to channel their competitive energies entirely into business by the time they reach middle management. A gathering of top business leaders might yield many insights into the activity of markets but would generate few into the richness of life beyond the markets. Indeed, one of the characteristics which defines business people is their healthy pragmatism. Of course in business people must have ideas and be comfortable with concepts and able to think in the abstract. No business would exist or flourish without continual refreshing of the strategy behind it and monitoring of that strategy in a changing environment. Business, however, is ultimately about products and services and is rooted, therefore, in the practical, the actual and those things which can be realized. Business people are not philosophers and do not have much call for rhetoric. There are always exceptions to every rule but I struggle to think of senior business figures who have found time to combine writing, art or music with a successful career in a corporation. Business does sometimes give people the freedom to return to any interests of this kind later in life. It is increasingly the case that senior executives will build a portfolio of non-executive roles which might include one not for profit position in an area where they have particular interests. The Royal Opera House, for example, is chaired by Sir Colin Southgate the former Chairman of Thorn EMI, while Gerry Robinson of Granada chairs the Arts Council. On the whole, however, observers can be forgiven for concluding that business is a rather soulless world.

The rewards

Business remains, however, a sphere which enables many to keep body *and* soul together. As a business leader you will hold the fate of, perhaps, many thousands or hundreds of thousands of people in your corporate hands. Business is the primary fuel for the global economy. The wealth generated by businesses enables the richness of life in other spheres. Those who question the motives of our leading business people neglect the power that businesses have to do immense good. A thriving business is one that employs people and provides, often directly through pension provision, security in the future. Businesses allow people to achieve balance in their lives, providing sufficient rewards to compensate for some of the privations of working life. Those in middle management in corporations may well earn well in excess of those at the top in some spheres of life, notably government administration or the voluntary sector, and so business liberates such people enabling them to make many more choices than their counterparts in other sectors. Indeed, business in recent years has created a cadre of very wealthy people (those who did reach the top) in their middle years who plough their personal profits back into enriching life for others, taking some of the skills acquired in business into other spheres for the general public good.

A business career may be intensely rewarding in many more ways than mere financial rewards. The solution of business problems can provide tremendous intellectual stimulation: how otherwise could business maintain the talents of so many intellectually able people, often the best graduates? In particular, business offers extraordinary opportunities to understand other cultures. While many businesses are domestic in outlook, many more are international and, increasingly global. It is possible to see the world, acquire numerous languages and broad-ranging cultural insights while working within just one corporation. Business both expands individual boundaries and collapses international ones as international executives work side by side in pursuit of a common goal: the success of the enterprise by which they are jointly employed. It may not be too absurd to say that international corporations enhance international understanding and minimize conflict by bringing together many nations and nationals under a single umbrella. This chance to work with and become close to people from a diverse range of countries and cultures can be truly exhilarating and offers an opportunity that in previous generations was more likely to come through the diplomatic and foreign services, an option open only to an élite few.

Open to all

Business is élitist in so far as it is interested in gaining the best results from the best people or, leveraging excellent management and leadership, the best results from the available people. Business, however, does not recognize many barriers and is truly a meritocracy. It is increasingly the case that business attracts graduates, but this fact is in part a reflection of expanding educational opportunities. Many businesses, through sponsorship and sandwich courses, support educational initiatives, and most provide opportunity without a ceiling to those who, for whatever reason, did not receive an education to match their ability. In view of the diversity of skills and experiences deployed in business there is also a great breadth of abilities that the business world can harness. While the very rounded person will prove the best general manager, business can prove stimulating and rewarding for people with one-sided skill sets. Indeed, business is an environment which can realise the potential of the many, satisfying the wildest dreams of the lucky few. Much has been written about the glass ceiling that has prevented equal numbers of women as men finding long-term senior careers in business. I will not deny that it is still easier for men than for women to reach the top, although some of this lies in the obsessive nature of business at the top which cannot always allow for a life outside. Even this is changing as businesses become much more dependent on women in senior positions and bound, therefore, to be flexible. New technologies can enhance the opportunities for people to combine executive and personal responsibilities. Business is, indeed, a great absorber of new technologies. The immediacy of others through mobile telephony and electronic communication has, to a certain extent, been brought about by the willingness of businesses to take up and extend new technologies, thereby turning remote scientific ideas into everyday realities in a miraculously short space of time.

Business is a broad term that I have used in a rather blanket fashion to date. Much of this book concerns itself with corporations, with the large (and sometimes not so large) established companies and their hierarchies. Such businesses offer scale and scope for ambitious young people but also very often offer the chance to achieve power without some of the risks attendant upon business start-ups. The corporate manager is a different beast from the entrepreneur. In order to succeed, both will need to be innovative, but entrepreneurs will risk far more in pursuit of their big ideas. The entrepreneur will found a business, will put his or her own money and future at stake and, in return for taking the bigger risk, can if all goes well expect to take out the bigger reward. In the following table I have, separately, characterized the differences between the business leader, the manager (one who is comfortable working within but probably not at the top of an entity) and the entrepreneur.

Leaders	Entrepreneurs	Managers
Charisma	Calculated risk	Analysis
Beguiling	Starting something	Cool
Vision	Building the new	Logical
Strategies	Independence	Process
Motivation of people	Game player	Systems
Catalyst for change	Iconoclast	Conservative
Inspiration	Not constrained	Planning
Energizing people	Everything is possible	Budgeting
The longer term	Focus	Controlling
Dreams	Energy	Problem solving
Big picture	Luck	Predictability
Empowerment	Tenacity	Frameworks
Cultural values	Creators of the new	Reduction of risk
Personality centred	Innovation	Rationality
Irrational	Unorthodox personality	Structures and rules
Drive		Detail
Originality		Build an organization

Source: John Viney, *Drive: Leadership in Business and Beyond* (Bloomsbury, 1999).

In a similar exercise, I have tried to consider some of the values and adjectives which describe business, set against those which describe the professions and the voluntary sector. In choosing whether business is really the appropriate market in which you can develop your personal brand it might be helpful to consider how comfortable you would feel with these values and to assess whether you want to be a corporate animal or whether you have ambitions to go it alone as an entrepreneur.

All of the above tries to give a big picture sense of the world of business, what it is and isn't, but how can you as an individual assess whether this is the place for you? For the remainder of this chapter I want to focus more on the values and skills of the

Business – corporate	Business – entrepreneurial	Public service	Professions	Voluntary service
Profit	Profit	Policy	Advisory	Welfare
Power	Power	Influence	Influence	Some influence/some power
Winning	Making the rules	Playing the game	Not losing	Changing the rules
Driven	Driven	Analytical	Theoretical	Caring
Verbal	Verbal	Written	Written and verbal	
Hierarchical	Autocratic	Hierarchical	Consensual	Bureaucratic
Risk	High risk	No risk	Low risk	No risk
Competitive	Passionate	Precise	Impartial	Conviction
Process	Vision	Procedure	Project	Continuum
Moderate	Maverick	Liberal	Conservative	Liberal
Persona	Personality	Impersonal	Versatility	Personal
Straightforward	Direct	Complex	Subtle	Complicated
Active	Pragmatic	Political	Conceptual	Practical
Timely	Speed	Enduring	Reactive	Responsive
Wealth	Riches	Moderation	Comfort	Reward
Ambition	Dreams	Position	Status	Worth
Focus	Compromise	Breadth	Flexibility	Campaigning

individual, some of which will fit better in a business world than others. What follows is largely a set of questions which should help you define your own 'brand' values.

Values

Ask a small child what they want to do when they grow up and you will be given an answer which falls, broadly, into one of two categories. Some children will want to be doctors, nurses, teachers, firefighters or police officers. Others will want to be popstars or footballers. The first group is attracted by the role. They want to occupy a position in society that is recognizable and valued. The second group is attracted by glory of a more sensational kind. They want fame and fortune – and, along the way, they want some fun. As we grow up we give more sophisticated answers to the question, but underpinning those answers are similar responses.

We start making choices very young. Some are made for us of course. We are given names which reflect the social and emotional aspirations and predilections of our parents. They shape us, position us in the eyes of all those we meet, just as does our style of dress, our religious and ethnic identity, and our class position. Children seldom choose their schools even if they may be consulted in the decision. However, at an early point the child is asked, in the British education system, to select subjects to pursue and subjects to dismiss. This process is refined to the point that the pupil must choose one or two subjects and perhaps a subsidiary subject to study at undergraduate level. Even at this early stage it is useful to take a careful approach to the decision. Most make the decision on the basis of what they enjoy and it usually follows that the subject enjoyed is one where the child has some ability and where the subject accords with their particular value system. A child who excels at drama, art and history of art is unlikely to want to be an engineer and probably does not see him/herself as a captain of industry, so the instinctive choice to study where ability and interest coincide is likely to be sensible. This is not the case for the child with a vocation – a desire, for example, to be a veterinary surgeon. He or she will be obliged to pursue a specific set of subjects in order to gain entry to the appropriate course. Those born with such a vocation are lucky; they are spared the indecision which dogs many of us. Alternatively, where the vocation requires a level of ability beyond the individual there can be considerable heartache ahead. Even at this early stage, then, it is advisable to find a match between aspiration, ability and values. These are obvious points but, at the core, is the strong sense that we should start thinking about what we really want, why we really want it and whether or not we are equipped to achieve it (and perhaps how we can better equip ourselves) at a young age. At the outset of your career you should be very open and honest with yourself.

There are some fundamental questions which, answered honestly, can help clarify the direction in which your career should tend.

What do you want to achieve in life?

- Fame and/or fortune
- Social standing
- Prestige
- Balance

- Respect
- Love

What would you like to leave behind you?

- A happy and stable family
- A reputation for having done something in the world, been somebody
- A sense that you have served others
- A sense of a life lived to the full

How would you like to be regarded by others?

- Successful
- Happy
- Creative
- Competent
- Active
- Thoughtful
- Practical
- Different
- Kind
- Driven

If you fail, what won't you have done?

- Fulfilled your potential
- Been true to yourself
- Enriched the lives of those around you
- Broken free from your roots
- Maintained the standard of living from which you came

How would you make the world a better place?

- By working to alleviate suffering
- By working to create opportunities for people

How comfortable are you:

- Doing something different from the herd?
- Being part of a community/team?

The above is a fairly random selection of important questions that point to one's values. I would expect a civil servant to give a different set of answers from an entrepreneur. Sometimes the answers may not be entirely palatable, but important issues to consider are:

- What value do you place on money? To what extent do you need material validation of your worth (smart clothes, fast cars, exotic holidays)?
- How ambitious/competitive are you? Are you naturally someone who must come first and always strives to beat your own and others' best?
- What are you prepared to give up in your life? Where will you make compromises? Must you always see the latest plays or will you work through the night if necessary? Is your home base important or do you yearn to travel?

As any schoolteacher will confirm, the greatest influence on our lives is the early home influence. In looking at the things that make up our value system, it is worth considering:

- To whom in your life do you naturally look up? What have they done and why?
- Who are your heroes in history, literature, sport? What, about them, do you admire?
- Who do you dislike? Are there any people for whom you have contempt? Why?

In interviewing candidates it is the motivation as much as achievements which one seeks to elicit. Indeed, achievements are very much easier to measure than the things which have made us who we are. As I discuss in a previous book there is a strong correlation between early hardship and later success. Loss of a parent or social disadvantage can provide individuals with the necessary drive to propel them to the top of their chosen profession. Career choices are very often made, not necessarily consciously, on the basis of early home experience. By way of example the following vignette is instructive.

The youngest of four brothers was the only one not to enter the medical profession, following in their father's footsteps. He studied all the relevant A levels but noted that his brothers were exhausted by punitive work schedules and disillusioned by the struggle to heal people to budget. He did not study medicine at university, but studied a mix of science and arts. He then chose to pursue a career in business much to the surprise of his family. Putting in similar hours as his brothers, he took out substantially greater financial rewards and developed a set of skills which he was later able to deploy for the public good. Having spent time in bank and then in a consultancy, he eventually took on a senior post in a not-for-profit organization where his skills and early value set enabled him to find fulfilment. His early decision was motivated by a recognition that he wanted to help make the world a better place but not at the cost of his own lifestyle. He knew that material things mattered to him. He also knew that the vision of public service which had motivated the decisions made by his brothers did not chime with the reality he saw lived by them. He dared to do something very different indeed and was ultimately able to make some money and to give something back.

It is worth examining closely what has made you who you are. Are you determined to break away from your background, or do you want to replicate it? What would you want your peer group to say of you? What would you wish your parents to think of you? How do you relate to your siblings? Deduce from your answers whether business really is the right place for you. If, as a younger child, you scorn the competitive style of your elders, relish observing and commentating on life more than engaging with it, loathe any group activities and want to be valued for the quality of your mind rather than the quantity of your deeds, then you will probably find business an uncongenial place. Alternatively, an only child whose childhood heroes were explorers and adventurers, who has loved the company of other children at school and in sport but retreated from them equally happily might well be at ease building a business and leading it. These are random and possibly glib examples, but understanding one's own experiences and psychology can make the difference between a good and bad decision.

On a light note, the following questionnaire may further illuminate your suitability for a career in business:

Business: will it make you or break you?

1.   You are playing a game of tennis and start to lose. Your opponent, usually weaker than you, cannot conceal his delight. Do you:

   (a) Shrug your shoulders and assume you are having a bad day and that you'll probably play better next time?

   (b) Take a decision not to face humiliating defeat, pick up your game and aim through a spectacular win to wipe the smile off your opponent's face, forcing him to conclude this was a new tactic?

   (c) Decide that if it matters to him to win that much you'll let him, and take pleasure in your magnanimity?

2.   Your final examinations are approaching. You have probably done enough work to get a good second but your tutor has suggested that with an extra spurt and considerable curtailment of your social life you could obtain a first. Do you:

   (a) Immediately cancel all social life and retreat into the library, emerging for the occasional cup of coffee and a few hours sleep?

   (b) Work out a schedule which allows for less socializing and more work in the hope that maintaining some balance will keep you fresh to face the exam questions on the day?

   (c) Conclude that all you need is a good second and if you are that close to a first your second is pretty secure so add a few extra hours socializing to an already packed week?

3. You are planning your holiday. Do you choose:

   (a) A European tour taking in the major cultural sites, accompanied by a close friend, a sketchbook and a pile of novels from the canon of European literature?

   (b) An adventure holiday, trekking through the Himalayas with an extended group of friends and friends of friends?

   (c) A week's course on watercolour painting in the heart of the countryside?

4. You have suddenly inherited £250,000 from an elderly aunt. Do you:

   (a) Set yourself up in a house knowing that you will be freed from worrying about mortgage payments for the foreseeable future?

   (b) Invest in the stock market, building a balanced portfolio but with some high-risk/high-reward options with a view to building a truly significant capital sum that you can really do something with?

   (c) Get embarrassed that you have come into such a large amount of money and make a few donations to your preferred charities, set aside money for the education of your children and invest the rest in high-interest accounts and premium bonds?

5. Your neighbour plays loud music at unsociable hours. The residents' committee are unsure how to deal with it. Do you:

(a) Suggest putting together a petition from all the residents in tandem with calling the local council to monitor the nuisance with a view to taking legal steps in due course?

(b) Tackle the problem directly with your neighbour, pointing out that if the residents committee is obliged to take action it could involve prosecution and a fine, and add that you have alerted your friend on the local paper who will be running a prominent piece on the perpetrators of noise nuisance?

(c) Insist on a co-ordinated vigilante response involving the collective playing of loud music at times when you know your neighbour is trying to sleep?

6. A headhunter calls you looking for candidates for an interesting and lucrative role. A close friend of yours with broadly relevant experience is looking for a job, but you have doubts about their calibre. Do you:

(a) Decide that the friendship matters more than anything else and give a glowing recommendation for the individual?

(b) Stay silent, you do not want to be judged by the headhunters on the basis of such a recommendation?

(c) Mention the friend but with the caveat that you cannot vouch for their ability?

7. You have employed a cleaner, a harassed single mother who needs the money. Within two or three weeks it is clear that she does not meet the standards you expect. Do you:

(a) Find an excuse to get rid of her, sending her on her way with a generous cheque?

    (b) Tell her that you are not happy with the standard of her work and ask her to make a concerted effort to improve or you will have to fire her?

    (c) Decide that she has enough pressures and at least the flat is cleaner than it would be if you had no cleaner?

8. Your department is doing some fundraising for a local charity. In a balloon debate there are three potential parts you can play. Do you choose:

    (a) Leonardo da Vinci?

    (b) Mahatma Gandhi?

    (c) Florence Nightingale?

9. At the office Christmas party the girlfriend of one of your staff gets drunk and decides to deliver some home truths to you. Do you:

    (a) Accept the staff member's apology gracefully and make a mental note to exclude partners in future years?

    (b) Accept the staff member's apology but suggest that some important issues have been surfaced that you want to clear up between you?

    (c) Avoid speaking to the staff member until after the Christmas holiday when you can safely pretend it never happened?

10. You get drunk at the Christmas party and deliver some home truths to your boss. Do you:

    (a) Apologize unreservedly and after a decent lapse of time ask for a transfer to another department?

    (b) Apologize unreservedly, express your deep regret at the manner in which you had surfaced your concerns but suggest that since they are now out in the open the two of you try and work through them in a mature fashion?

(c) Call in sick and go straight to the job centre, only returning to the office to resign?

No Bs at all – Forget it. Business is your nightmare.

Some Bs – It's possible that you will find a niche in business, but you should look more widely too.

Mainly Bs – Business is your natural home. Head for the corporate sector right now.

Skills

Values matter in the choices you make, but skills are also a vital factor in the equation. Few people entering the workforce have the skills needed to achieve success in whichever walk of life it is they have chosen. Even a brilliantly educated barrister will need the benefit of experience to turn extensive theory into practical virtuosity. Specific vocational skills will usually be supplied by employers. Hence large corporations offer excellent graduate training schemes while the civil service has its fast-stream entry, both designed to take raw potential and to shape it into fully formed talent. There are a set of skills, however, which are not directly task related but connected with personality and inclination. These are perhaps better styled as traits or attributes. Understanding what these are can clarify the course one's career should take. Some of the areas where interviewers, consciously or not, will focus are:

• Do you enjoy abstract thought?

- Are you more comfortable with detail and concrete examples?
- Are you expansive and do you think in broad terms?
- Are you intensive focusing on a smaller area in depth?
- Are you as comfortable with numbers as with words?
- Do you prefer to deconstruct or to build, are you a critic or a creator?
- How comfortable are you giving instruction?
- Do you need to be loved?
- Can you tolerate being respected but not liked?
- Do you need to be part of a team?
- Are you comfortable working in isolation?
- Do you enjoy accomplishing tasks with a beginning, middle and end?
- Do you lose interest after the initial phase of a project or task?
- Would you rather be seen as someone who acts or someone who thinks?

These questions are aids to thought and self-definition and there is no immediately right or wrong answer. The Chief Executives of our top corporations are not a homogenous and uniform group but come from very diverse backgrounds and bring a mix of skills – for the sake of enterprise, we must hope that this will continue to be the case. In general, however, Chief Executives must be self-aware and as good a judge of themselves as they are of others. They should be comfortable making judgements and taking the necessary steps to right any wrongs they find. They should be prepared to make decisions which will be painful for others in the interests of the greater good. To do so they must be prepared to be unpopular sometimes and under scrutiny at all times. They must also be prepared to be accountable. The Chief Executive of a major business has extraordinary power. Despite all the checks and balances that are in place to prevent a business from misrule by any one autocratic individual it will always be the case that the person at the head of a business has a terrifying capacity to mastermind its salvation, secure its strong future or wreak its ultimate destruction. In doing any of these things the Chief Executive will affect the lives of all those working in the business or in those enterprises which depend on it, as well, of course, as those who invest in it. Companies can make or break the opportunities for those working with them currently and those who will work with them in the future and a failed company can have a shattering effect on local (and not so local) economies just as a successful organization can create a meta-economy in its own locale. Arguably, the head of a corporation can have more influence than any one individual since the days of city-states and their princely heads. Indeed, the anti-globalization protesters resist the global corporation precisely because they see this parallel. In truth, the corporate Chief Executive, while not elected by those he or she leads, is nevertheless seldom self-imposed and always subject to the harshest criticism from the severest judges: the markets and those who invest in them. The responsibilities are vast and the scope for failure at least as great as that for success. The most successful business leader may be respected but is unlikely to be seen as a hero. The unsuccessful business leader, on the other hand, can expect to be publicly pilloried. It is by no means certain that the rewards to Chief Executives *do* compensate for the risks and responsibilities, not to mention the personal sacrifices. All too often the power of the Chief Executive comes at an extremely high personal price. Do you still dream of being a Chief Executive? The vertigo-prone among you will have ceased reading, but those with a head for heights should read on . . .

CHAPTER 2

The value of education and early career choices

Laying the foundations for future success. The value of formal education to the corporate aspirant or the entrepreneur. Choosing an institution, choosing a course, choosing a career, choosing a company – what to ask. Returning to education. The MBA. Assessing progress, what should you achieve in the early years of your career?

Some of you may have read the title of this chapter with a slight sinking of the heart. Is the author about to insist on a single conservative career path to the top in business? One of the strengths of the commercial sector has been its ability to embrace all comers, with the single proviso that they have the talent to make money or to contribute to the making of money and the integrity to do so legally and ethically. A cursory look at the boards of the United Kingdom's top 250 companies by market capitalization will show that corporate business leaders spring from a range of sources and are variously educated, some combining top schools with top universities, others having no tertiary education at all and only modest secondary experience. Some will have acquired their knowledge of business not through any formal education but, perhaps, through observing their parents running small businesses. Indeed, a study of entrepreneurially led businesses would show a fairly consistent absence of university education. Bill Gates, Richard Branson and the late Jimmy Goldsmith eschewed university, although the latter two did so having acquired the confidence that can come from the British public school system. Bill Gates (who spent a term or so at Harvard) perhaps had the confidence that derives from having a great idea? Really successful entrepreneurs, those who found large businesses, tend to be driven by extraordinary energy and are disinclined to hang around acquiring qualifications which are of dubious benefit when set against that innate drive and ambition. Indeed, too much education can have the effect of eroding confidence and the dare-devil spirit of seeing 'What if . . . ?'

Only a handful of individuals in each generation will have the skills, personality, luck and opportunities to create world-class businesses from scratch. Fewer still have the ability to spot future trends and circumvent the need for education. Indeed, in recent years when technology stocks have stood very high a number of people have amassed great fortunes through business initiatives founded on the basis of scientific/intellectual endeavour – think of the businesses that have come out of MIT or Cambridge University. Indeed, the city of Cambridge's high-tech success has created more than 400 multimillionaires out of a population of only 110,000, and many of these are likely to become angel investors, financing their friends to become entrepreneurs. Education has, for some, been the passport to entrepreneurial success. Take David Potter, founder and now Chairman of Psion. He came from an academic family: his grandfather was a Professor of Civil Engineering and his grandmother was the first women to graduate from Cape Town University. Potter collected a series of qualifications, including a Ph.D. in theoretical physics, and spent some years in the groves of academe before he founded Psion. He founded the business, by the way, using funds made through judicious playing of the markets. Such entrepreneurs are, perhaps, the product of a certain moment in history and almost the antithesis of the classic entrepreneurial profile. Indeed, Potter is paradigmatic of the happy confluence of opportunity and talent, and it is no small coincidence that the later period of his academic career was spent on the west coast of America. It is also of note that, somewhat atypically of the products of the British or, indeed, Commonwealth education system, Potter is something of an outsider: he lost his father at fourteen and came to the UK to complete his education from South Africa. In general, where fortunes are made on the back of academic careers they are made on the back of highly successful postgraduate careers, rather than undergraduate careers. Perhaps such people are driven, in the first instance, by a desire to generate a successful idea which has, almost as a by-product, turned into the creation of a successful business by way of making that idea available as widely as possible. In general, these examples notwithstanding, education *per se* is unlikely to be the single root of success.

Education, all the same, achieves many things. For some it is a means of buying time, for others a way of breaking out of home. Some have a passion for scholarship, others for sport and choose to spend three, sometimes four years indulging these. Many people make their most intense and enduring friendships while they are students and most experiment with different personae. The experience of tertiary education is, by and large, a positive one for most people. Indeed, universities and colleges offer many a laboratory or, perhaps, a studio in which the young (or not so young) can work on themselves, defining the formula for their particular personality, sculpting themselves into a shape they are happy for the world to see.

The intent of this chapter is not to proscribe a particular form of education which will, more than any other, enable future Chief Executives to take their first steps towards their goal. It is to look at the importance of early choices in the production of one's personal brand. The choice of subject, university and college is perhaps the first decision that you will make independently. You may well receive advice, but the ultimate decision will be your own. You will be judged as much by the decision you make as by the use you make of it. Most employers must use a filter when they recruit young people. The obvious one is educational achievement since education offers a ready yardstick by which to judge people. That being the case, it is worth making the most of the facility. The second major choice, of company or career direction which this chapter will go on to consider, will be influenced by success in the first. I would take issue with those who think that a mistake at this stage can undermine an entire life. There are always steps we can take to right early wrong decisions (and grow by so doing), but as with all things if we can avoid making mistakes, it is advisable to do so.

Yet choosing a university or college can be daunting, especially where students have only a hazy idea of what they want to do, beyond having a good time. Seventeen- and eighteen-year-olds face a bewildering array of choices and often rather limited advice. Parental agendas can interfere with decision-making and teachers' experience of the world is very often limited to the schoolroom. In both cases, advice may reflect the practices and prejudices of their own generation. Many parents who would not have considered entering business during the 1960s or 1970s when making their own choices cannot adequately advise their own children on how they should prepare themselves in the event that business is their chosen field. It is not, for example, sensible simply to suggest that a business studies course will equip a student for a business career. There is no substitute, after all, for real practical experience of business. Alternatively, it is increasingly the case that successful business people offer interesting role models to their children who are able to make informed choices in their late teens and early twenties.

Choosing a subject – does it matter?

I want to spend a few moments considering the purpose of education. One of the simplest mistakes to make is to assume it is about the acquisition of knowledge. Of course, it would be facile to suggest that learning facts does not have its part to play in the development of rounded personalities, but any student will testify to the impossibility of retaining much beyond the outline facts of their subjects. Education, at the higher levels, in any case, is as much about form as it is about content. It is a commonplace that a degree demonstrates a certain level of skills and a capacity to learn, concentrate and, perhaps, a certain amount of organization and maturity.

There are particular skills and attributes which some forms of study will develop to a greater extent than others. Some subjects are primarily about taking a problem and solving it through the application of rigorous logic without reference beyond the problem itself. Some subjects are based on precedent or bring together a body of work where in order to be original oneself one must show cognisance of the best ideas others have had. Some subjects will be more insular than others, where debate will not necessarily improve the outcome. Others are much more discursive and emotive. The clearest and easiest distinction to be drawn is between numeracy and literacy. Compare the length of a doctoral thesis in an arts to a science subject. In choosing a subject consider your own inclinations; what have you enjoyed or excelled at in school? Are you comfortable in a debate or did you prefer solitary study and problem solving? Do you enjoy tremendous focus or are you more comfortable with a broad-ranging subject? (See table on next page.)

The subject chosen matters little for its content. What counts is the skills you will acquire in the course of your study. I can think of several very able business people who studied theology, an apparently unlikely choice. When, however, one considers that the subject draws on history, archaeology, anthropology, linguistics, philosophy, politics and geography (to name but a few examples), it becomes clear that this is a subject requiring tremendous ability to synthesize and, importantly, a holistic and broad approach. These are not bad skills

Skill associated with different subjects

	Problem solving	Logic	Collation	Distillation/ synthesis	Simplifying	Judgement/ intuition	Numeracy	Literacy	Communi- cation
Maths	•	•		•	•		•		
Engineering	•	•		•	•		•		
Physics	•	•	•		•		•		
Chemistry	•	•			•	•	•		
Biology			•	•		•			
Languages			•	•		•		•	•
Literature			•	•		•		•	•
History		•	•	•	•	•		•	•
Human sciences	•					•			
Law		•	•	•	•	•			•
Medicine	•		•			•			•

for business. Similarly, classics. The study of physics involves the ability to take tremendous imaginative leaps, to think the unthinkable, to coin a current business buzz phrase, and is entirely consistent with developing strategies for companies. Lawyers will naturally have a close eye for detail which perhaps is likely to feature in the linguist's toolkit, but the linguist might have a better ear for nuance than, say, the chemist. Some disciplines equip people for particular business activities. Is it accident that a number of strategy consultants have engineering degrees? I doubt it. Rather the multitask, multidisciplinary nature of engineering, with its overt focus on problem solving, is broadly similar to the day-to-day tasks of a consultant.

Of course, on one level this is purely fanciful. Some would say that one academic discipline is much like another, requiring an ability to research, learn, debate, draw conclusions and prove a case. All the same, there are differences and it is worth considering the skills with which you will emerge, especially if you are one of the bold souls who decides to take a leap in the dark and study something that you have not studied in school. For those preparing for a career in business (or wanting to leave their options open) I would strongly advocate the study of a fairly traditional subject, one that can be widely understood and which has a degree of gravitas. A historian is likely to be taken seriously intellectually more widely than, for example, a sports scientist. Business admires hard work, and subjects that require you to work to tight deadlines and to produce well-researched pieces in a timely and efficient manner can give a headstart. Those disciplines which require the marshalling of facts and the proving and disproving of theories can give an edge in dealing with disciplines outside one's own, by providing a framework for probing and questioning. Indeed, education is just that – a framework or skeleton on which you can add flesh.

Choosing an institution

Choosing the right subject is, of course, only part of the decision. Unless you pursue a vocational subject as a mandatory requirement of your preferred occupation, the subject you have chosen is likely to have been forgotten rather sooner than the institution you attended or the grade you attained. This is where branding starts to matter. Whether we like it or not there is a hierarchy of educational establishments the world over, with some being more highly regarded than others. Reputations, bad or good, are not always deserved or accurate but perceptions are slow to change and a good institution will attract good students and good teachers, and a bad one (to put it crudely) will attract less good students and less good lecturers. Aim high, choose the toughest course in the best university that you can and give yourself access to a broad range of influences and testing peers.

Consider a scenario where two people of equal ability attend two very different institutions. The first receives excellent advice and goes to a top university where her peers are articulate, able and ambitious and she must fight to keep up with or ahead of the pack. The second is ill-advised and chooses an institution on the basis of location. She habitually out-ranks her peers with ease and takes a very good degree, but not the outstanding one she might have done. Both start work in the same organization. The first is entirely comfortable with her peers, and adjusts to the standards quickly. She makes her mark on the graduate training programme with the effortlessness which comes from custom. The second, for the first time, finds herself surrounded by people who are as good as she. Her confidence sinks, her performance dips and she is much slower to realize the potential her employers had initially identified in her. At the end of the day the second can, with sufficient drive, catch up – but she has made it a little harder for herself and will have created a less than excellent impression – and perception is important. It may be that she will need to move on to another organization to establish herself with the benefit of this lesson learned. If there is one message I would deliver on the basis of long years of studying the successful it would be this: align yourself with the best.

Education and confidence

Education can give tremendous confidence and confidence is the closest we may come to an elixir of success. Someone commented to me recently about a young woman they had known at 17 or 18. When they were next introduced to her at 25 she was scarcely the same woman at all. She had matured and acquired confidence simply by dint of finding something at which she genuinely excelled. She had come to this point through education. Set against this, however, the experience of the brilliant pupil whose zenith comes when they collect their first. Education can give confidence but, where it is not supported by an ability to exist in the world, may end up having only given false confidence or, at least, false hope.

I would venture to suggest that a formal education is of far more importance to the individual with corporate ambitions than it is to the would-be entrepreneur. The structures of formal education, the process of learning (tutorials and seminars) and the spirit of friendly rivalry between those studying the same subject are an excellent preparation for corporate life and give a solid basis of achievement from which to launch a career. Education can be a great leveller and the child from the underprivileged background may, by dint of achievement, acquire some of the confidence of the comfortably middle-class, but perhaps less able, child.

Confidence is often the greatest asset that an entrepreneur has. This confidence may take the form of a certain stubbornness, and a self belief that enables them to take their own counsel and stand by their own decisions. I am struck when considering entrepreneurs, how many have not pursued their education to university, and largely through choice. Mark Dixon, the founder of Regus left school after acquiring nine O levels confident that he could make his way in the world and not wanting to delay his progress by unnecessary study, of which he would have been easily capable. Charles Dunstone, the founder of Carphone Warehouse had a place to read business studies at Liverpool University but during his gap year came to the conclusion he would rather go out and found businesses than study them. Essex boys both, Dixon and Dunstone come from rather different backgrounds. Dixon's is humble, his father was a mechanic and his mother a housewife. Dunstone's father, in contrast, was a BP executive and was able to educate his son at public school (Uppingham). Both Dixon and Dunstone disdained university because they were in a hurry – and because they already had tremendous confidence. Perhaps Dixon's was the confidence of the able person who has not been raised in an environment that particularly sets store by educational attainment, whereas Dunstone had the confidence that comes from good connections and, fundamentally, some wealth behind him. It is certainly intriguing to note that in the recent internet boom some of the most celebrated (or notorious) entrepreneurs were those who had been public school educated and combined both innate self confidence and a sense that their personal risks could be cushioned by family wealth. Lastminute.com's Brent Hoberman and Martha Lane-Fox were both educated at public schools (Eton and Westminster respectively) although both trod a traditional path by then taking degrees at Oxford. My intention is not to make any particular points about privilege – privilege without talent counts for little, after all – but to emphasize the importance of confidence in the business world. In the risky world of the entrepreneur confidence is, quite simply, essential.

Missing out on education

Perhaps you are now in your late twenties or early thirties. You know you were meant for better things than the rather humdrum job you have, but – for whatever reason – did not acquire a particularly good education and nor did you demonstrate great energy, passion and confidence at a young age. All the same, you want to be a Chief Executive, you want to run something. Is it too late for you? Martha Lane-Fox, as you know all too well, was only in her middle twenties when she first shot to prominence and Brent Hoberman was very little older. Is there still hope for you? My task in this book is to try and shed light and suggest options rather than to shut them down. The entrepreneurs mentioned above have shown exceptional courage, tenacity and talent and have had a reasonable amount of good fortune along the way. Theirs is not the only way to achieve success, however, and, provided you dream the dream badly enough and have sufficient conviction in your own abilities, you should be able to turn a slow start to good advantage. The internet boom and the rise of distance learning will enable increasing numbers to participate in education as mature students. Universities compete for mature students who swell the coffers and employers respect the sacrifices involved in returning to full-time education. They respect the determination to create opportunities. Perhaps you can bypass an academic education in favour of a more practical one, taking one of the numerous MBA courses on offer. Or maybe if you still feel uncomfortable with the notion of spending time in education but want to become involved in a corporation you should consider environments where the prevailing culture is action-orientated. Perhaps the world of retailing would offer you scope and enable you to acquire formal management training?

Education – so what?

A recent headline by Julie Burchill, an outspoken newspaper columnist, declared: 'Want to be an original, interesting person? Then don't bother going to university.' I am a recepient and strong advocate of education. All the same I can sympathize with those who feel it is overrated and for those disappointed A level students who miss out each year there is no reason to feel entirely down-hearted. Universities can have negative consequences as well as positive. In particular, they reinforce hierarchies and insert difference where there need be none. Many people feel that a university education is a guarantor of success, not an aid to success. They become complacent, believe themselves to be of greater worth by dint of a piece of paper cataloguing achievements in just three short years. This complacency undermines success far faster than the absence of a degree. Education as a cushion is the theme of comments made recently by entrepreneur John Madekski who sold his publishing company in 1998 for £260 million: 'Too many young people define themselves in terms of academic achievements, and they aren't prepared to get their hands dirty when they go into the world of work. My own lack of paper qualifications actually helped me in business. With no safety net I simply had to succeed.'

The phrase 'ivory tower' is frequently used of academic institutions. Most universities are more attuned to the real world than in previous generations, but they remain insular, cloistered and in numerous cases uncomfortable with business and business people. A good student and potential Chief Executive might find himself dissuaded, albeit passively, from pursuing a business career because of the more overtly public spirited, less profit driven values which pertain in most higher educational institutions. Universities operate at a considerable remove from the real world. A classic reason why people do not go to university is that they want to start earning money as soon as possible and take their place in that real world. Given that making money is the *raison d'être* behind most businesses it is perhaps insane that we have any prejudice against those for whom money is such an overt motivation.

Education and access

Education is probably, ultimately, far more relevant for those with corporate than with entrepreneurial ambitions. For this population education can give access as well as confidence. Most corporations of significant size or prestige invest heavily in securing the services of the best graduates. They will have a hierarchy of institutions which they know habitually generate individuals with the skill-sets to suit their particular industry. They will also have a well defined sense of the personality type that fits the corporation. Natural entrepreneurs tend to fit themselves rather better than they fit a corporate entity. Corporations will woo their candidate pool and, not for the first time, the soon-to-be graduate finds him or herself confronting another enormous decision and often imperfect data on which to make it. For some the decision is not a difficult one at all. They know they want to go into a media company or arts administration, the civil service or education. There are, however, a huge number of opportunities which may not come under consideration for the simple reason that they lack visibility. Here is the final year student's opportunity to put their research skills to good use and find out what their options really are. Once the obvious things like the careers advisory service have been exhausted, what should the uninitiated student, with a vague feeling that they would like to be in business, do next?

Analysing the opportunities

- Pool intelligence with your friends and peers. What have they discovered? Are there certain options that you can immediately eliminate?

- What have people who studied the same course as you in previous years gone on to do? Can you make contact with them? Can you build a picture of what it is they do and how it would correspond to your own interests and skills?

- Are your parents, your parents' friends or even your friends' parents involved in the business world. Can they talk you through your options? Can they perhaps make introductions to different organizations so that you can assess the reality of the work environment?

- When offered formal interviews by organizations take advantage of the forum to understand as much as you can about the company, and about the different roles within it. If you move into marketing, what will that mean? Or finance? Or human resources? Think medium as well as short-term.

Once you have a feel for a particular sector, set about understanding the dynamics of that sector.

Who are the key players? Which are the most successful? Is that success a flash in the pan? What are the factors that make companies successful (great brand, strong processes, brilliant people)? As you begin to gain a sense of what the business world is about you will be able to assess yourself against it and particular companies against your own requirements.

Find a match between yourself and a corporation

- Will you feel more comfortable in a large, small or medium sized environment. Do you get a buzz from scale, or feel insignificant when confronted by a vast multi-national?

- Are you in a hurry? Do you want to move up the hierarchy fast? Is a fast growth, but higher risk company a better prospect than a traditional mature but first rate business with many first rate people competing for the same opportunities?

- How important is it for you to be in an international environment? How prepared are you to disrupt your personal life regularly in order to move with opportunities?

- Do you need to identify strongly with the product, or are you intrigued by the unknown?

- Have you seen people in the areas that you are beginning to focus on who impress you? Are there any you would aspire to emulate?

- Is there evidence of choice and progression. What have previous graduate intakes gone on to do? Do they remain in the company or take their training and run?

- Is the training the best you will find?

- How have you been treated? Are you a commodity or a potentially valuable resource?

- Can you see yourself in the people who are trying to recruit you?

- Can you define certain core values that appear common to all those you have met? Are they consistent with your own? Can the people you have met define core values they have in common and seek in others?

- What perceptions do others have regarding the organization that interests you? Is it one of the small group of businesses offering one of the best training opportunities, or is it seen to be second tier player?

Still not sure?

At the end of this process you may still feel uncertain. Perhaps no single company or activity has inspired you as you had expected but, still you think you would like to be involved in the private sector in some capacity. Perhaps this is the point at which to consider deferring the decision? An excellent mechanism by which to do just that is to enter consultancy or accountancy. These are professions which offer insight into the business world and, often, accelerated entry once qualifications have been gained or a certain level attained. The best consultancies and accounting firms set out to recruit people who will fuel their partnership, but most are sanguine about the inevitable departure of some post qualification, particularly where the departure may be to a client firm. Perhaps you find the very size and scale of major corporations off-putting. You may prefer being a bigger fish in a smaller pond and would benefit from joining a smaller company as a graduate trainee. You may find yourself the only graduate trainee and could gain greater exposure to a wider part of the business than your peers who choose the big company route.

Personal branding

Whether clear on this first choice or not, it is imperative that the would-be Chief Executive not lose sight of his/her own personal brand. This decision is not necessarily the most important you will make – but it will be there on your CV in perpetuity and will inevitably have some influence on the course the rest of your career will take. This is not the moment to compromise. Choose an organization that adds lustre to your own brand. Large corporations align themselves with the best service suppliers. A publicly quoted company will ensure that it has truly blue-chip advisers for its legal, accounting, consulting and advertising needs. You should ensure that your name is allied to one that is worthy of it. People very often make the choice of their first job, or first company on the basis of the people they have met and liked. This simple litmus test is a fairly reliable one – but an aspiring Chief Executive who finds himself in a business with terribly nice people going nowhere will either have to relinquish the dream, or the job. Look closely at the people, the environment and imagine yourself there:

- Are there people in the organization who will guide and steer you? Does the organization foster mentoring?
- What adjectives describe the people you have met? Would you like them to be applied to you?
- Imagine in three years time you are writing your CV. How would you be able to describe your job? What achievements can you anticipate? What can you learn?

Is it working? Does it matter?

This is your first job. For some it may be the company where you will spend your working life. Indeed, if you want to be the Chief Executive of a major domestic business it may well be that the company you join on graduating will be the company that you remain in for many years. Equally, it may not be. All manner of things can go wrong or, not go as right as you would like them to. Perhaps you dislike the sector, the location, the size of the business. Possibly you do not find it challenging. If you do not find that you are learning and stretched by the experience of work this is possibly the case. Perhaps you feel the organization is channelling you away from the skills you most wish to extend. Whatever the reason, you should not despair. Perhaps you are already in your late twenties reading this with a CV which shows that you have already shifted jobs several times in search of one that suits? Again, this is not cause either for despair or undue regret. The early days of a career are important in so far as they set the foundations for later success but, provided you can justify your decisions some wrong choices need not destroy your opportunities for the future – provided you exercise careful judgement and, in so far as possible, are consistent.

Perhaps you are blissfully happy in your first job? You may find that the people you find yourself among are congenial and the tasks you are called upon to execute are easily within your compass. Possibly you are earning a decent salary and can afford a relatively affluent lifestyle. This may be a dangerous position to find yourself in. Complacency is the enemy of success. It is not enough to dream of being a Chief Executive, you need to be sure that you are putting in place the skills and experiences which will make others think you worthy of the position. Throughout your career you need to monitor progress, just as a marketeer will test market a brand, seek constant market feedback and refine the brand strategy in order to maximize its success, considering the channel strategy, the packaging and the success of the brand relative to its rivals.

Checklist for early career steps

- How are you performing relative to your peer group? Are you keeping up with those who joined at the same time, surging ahead or falling behind?

- When the time comes to be given a new assignment are you allocated to a function or division which has high standing in the business or are you lost in the crowd?
- What is your progress relative to your peers from school/college/university?
- Do you have a sense of the hurdles you need to leap over to secure the next step?
- Are you paying attention to your weaknesses or merely looking for recognition of your strengths?
- Are you monitoring those ahead of you and identifying what it takes to be successful in your chosen environment?
- Do you fit with the culture? Too well? Not well enough?
- What level of visibility have you achieved with people senior to yourself? Are any showing signs of interest in mentoring you?
- Are you keeping pace with your own expectations for yourself? Are these in keeping with those that others have for you.

Most large organizations have mechanisms for enabling the company and employees to assess progress. You should use the forum of the appraisal to air your concerns and to voice your aspirations but, importantly, to listen to feedback. One of the greatest skills in the armoury of a Chief Executive is the ability to listen, learn and act upon the lessons learnt. Consider the advice you are given. Consider, too, the person who is giving that advice. As I have said previously, align yourself with the best. If one of the stars of the generation a level above you suggests that your vocal objections to a particular policy are counterproductive and that a reasoned demonstration of your viewpoint would be better received you should take note. The message here is that your objections may be valid, but the means of delivery undermines their validity. If, on the other hand, a rather militant and only averagely successful colleague suggests that you are making yourself unpopular by working at the weekends to ensure you are on top of your workload, they probably do not have your best interests at heart.

Puzzling the corporate maze

Entering the workplace can be a difficult time for anyone. New graduates who have been wooed extensively arrive in their new company only to find that they are the bottom of the heap and that all their previous glory counts for nothing. Those who have experienced company life during a gap year or in their vacations may have the advantage of seeing how companies work (and indeed we might add this experience to the useful research to be done while deciding on an appropriate choice of career). Those with no previous experience may be disorientated. Companies can be microcosms of the world and will hire people of mixed ability and varying motives. The newly arrived graduate trainee will need to operate across these different groups and, very often, will depend on some of the less talented, less highly motivated individuals in the corporate whole to achieve their own objectives. Plotting a course through the labyrinth of a company is no easy task and requires vigilance and cool, dispassionate judgement. It also requires the suspension of undue emotion.

One very able young woman I remember interviewing experienced a baptism of fire when she entered a business for the first time. She had been raised in a very affluent family and sent to excellent schools where she had mixed with people of similar class. She took the unusual step, amongst her peers, of studying engineering but then in a more conservative move, applied to a consultancy. For one of her first assignments she was sent to an Australian construction company to identify the reasons for a sharp decline in the number of contracts issued to the business (a division of a major international company) and the falling safety record. A slight and pretty girl, she arrived on a construction site, dressed for the office in a skirt and high heels. She was met with a mix of disbelief, scorn and harassment. She resolutely stuck to her principles, continued to go to work as if she were in a major metropolis and set about conducting the research, interviewing the principal players in the business and recording her results as if oblivious to the initial response. She took immense care to be accurate and respectful. She neither passed comment, nor shared confidences. She won the respect of the most hardened of the construction people, who admired her guts and her integrity. Arguably, she had it easier than if she were an employee of the company since she could take refuge in the fact that she was a representative of a third party. All the same, she was obliged to spend six months of her life in this alien community and, to all intents and purposes, was a member of that company. She remained true to herself, never lost sight of her objectives and asserted her authority by the simple expedient of never engaging with others on emotive subjects.

This story begs the question, what were her employers doing sending her on a case which seemed so unlikely to play to her strengths? The simple answer is that they were testing her.

They took a calculated risk based on a careful assessment of her character and personality. She had chosen her employer as well as they had chosen her; it was an environment that exercised tremendous judgement in the selection and deployment of staff.

The balance between the personal and the professional

One of the hardest lessons to learn if one is to be successful in business is that the professional and the personal do not mix well together. A graduate trainee comes fresh from an environment where she or he has been encouraged to explore their innermost being, their motivations, desires, troubled psyche and quirks of genetic inheritance (the laboratory of self, or studio to which I referred at the outset of this chapter). Business is interested in taking the outcomes of this understanding, but is not concerned with continued exploration. Business is steadfastly about action and contemplation is better enganged in away from the workplace. Of course it is by no means the case that all graduates have spent their studies indulging in intimate conversations about themselves. Many have used the time to produce plays, to play sport and to engage in student politics. In some ways, this community will find the transition into corporate life easier. They are accustomed to working with groups – albeit in play – and, in some cases, are proficient at giving instruction. They have the advantage of having mechanisms for detaching the personal from the professional. Those who have not attended university at all may have a distinct advantage when it comes to the requirement to split the public and private personae. The person who leaves school after O levels for instance, has been concerned with action, with working, and is likely to have a fairly no-nonsense approach. Too much self-knowledge can, ultimately be a handicap.

Management

Learning to manage is an important skill that the budding Chief Executive needs to acquire. There is an implicit irony in this statement. It is my firm belief that a really strong Chief Executive should lead rather than manage. It is also a cherished tenet of mine that management and leadership can very often be mutually exclusive. Leaders are concerned with vision, dreams, with enthusing others, with communicating a message and energizing a team. Managers, on the other hand, are concerned with process, with measuring, with control and balance. Unless, however, you plan to set up your own enterprise, you will not progress far in an organization unless you can acquire the basic skills of management. I struggle to think of people who have spent an entire career leading, enthusing and energizing but have never run anything, managing the transition to the role of Chief Executive. Consider, for example, the paradigm of the BBC. There are some brilliant creative minds in the organization who are critical to its success. They embody the spirit of the organization and enable able programme makers to find the best in themselves and so make outstanding programmes. Such people may contribute to the vision for the corporation but could not lead it as Director General because they lack balance, appetite for trivia, ability to engage in the mundane, in short to consider the day-to-day. The Chief Executive needs to understand management, to have experienced it and to have moved beyond it. He or she needs to know how to deploy others with brilliant management skills to take care of those tasks so as to focus on the tasks of leadership. The route to recognizing outstanding management is to have tried it oneself. To become a leader you do not need to be the best manager but you need to be a good enough manager.

Managing what?

This chapter is about early choices. One of the choices you need to make is to step into a position that offers you breadth of management tasks. It is increasingly the case that large corporations bring budding executive talent into the centre, put high potential young stars into important marketing or corporate strategy roles to give them access to the decision making processes, to see how it is done. Some find it exhilarating to be close to power. The Assistant to the Chairman or to the Chief Executive is a marvellous vantage point from which to understand the dynamics of a corporation and to come to understand what success in that organization actually entails. Knowing when to step away from the centre and to let go of the coat-tails of the powerful is a skill indeed. To stay in such a role beyond a couple of years is professional suicide for the would-be Chief Executive. It simply is not enough to sit in judgement of those making live and difficult decisions. The most brilliant critic will be inconsequential if he or she cannot prove that they can practice what they preach. Again and again I find there is no better way of proving a point than through action. In the early years of your career you need to ensure that you gain exposure to management of a variety of issues, among them:

- Management of people
- Management of budgets
- Management of time

- Management of external organizations, be they suppliers, customers or advisers
- Management of processes
- Management of relationships

If, by the time you reach your late twenties, you have not amassed experiences of this type you probably need to examine why that is. Management involves suspension of self and adherence to a set of values bigger than the individual. Of course, it is to be hoped that no decisions will be vastly at variance with an individual's personal moral system. Indeed, the successful manager must cling to their own integrity and ensure that they are ethical in their dealings at all times. Ethical – but not too emotional. As you become more successful you may find you have to make decisions that are not to the advantage of all the people around you. Perhaps an early boss of yours cherishes a particular scheme. You may have sat in a bar and listened to them expound their theory but, put in a position of authority over them, you know that that theory is unworkable and inadvisable. In such situations it is painful to disappoint. You may need to tolerate incurring wrath, dislike and a sense of betrayal on the part of the individual who has possibly been an important factor in your progression to date. Such situations require tact, diplomacy and an iron will. Strength of purpose and conviction in a given course of action are of incalculable benefit at such times.

Do you still like yourself?

Management is difficult. Regular terms of commendation in business are 'tough…fair…judicious'. These do not necessarily sit well with such terms as 'kindness…feeling…giving'. Successful managers will nurture talented people but they will do so on the basis of results. They will set people up so that they can fulfill their potential, but they will not be forgiving of repeated poor returns. You may find yourself working with someone who you know to be extremely bright. Perhaps they have given you some excellent ideas, some focused criticism or flashes of insight which have helped you solve problems. You may feel respect and gratitude towards them. If, however, they repeatedly let you down on particular assignments, make mistakes in dealing with people, or undermine your authority in some way you will be obliged to forsake your allegiance to them in favour of more reliable performers. In business you can afford to be generous only up to a point. You cannot afford to lose sight of the unifying principle that brings you together, the requirement to make profits on behalf of the enterprise. You can like people, but you may need to like them independently of judging and assessing their relevance to the organization.

In Chapter 1 I suggested that business can be harsh. In this chapter I am demonstrating precisely how, even in the opening chapters of your career, that harshness can be manifested. It may be the case that you find the requirement to judge people in these ways abhorrent or, at least, somewhat distasteful. Once you have tasted management you need to look closely at yourself and assess whether you have the appetite to continue. What do your friends think of you? Your girlfriend or boyfriend? During the course of your twenties you will change and develop considerably. Some lucky couples will develop at a similar pace, sharing experiences and values. Others will find that youthful altruism gives way to mature pragmatism in one partner but not in the other. Perhaps the partner you met at university starts to use terms like ruthless, where you would use terms like tough, to consider the decisions that you have made rationally to be unkind and uncaring. These judgements are important and you will need to assess them carefully. Possibly the judgements are accurate and a timely reminder that you have misunderstood the principles of management, and in your over-ambition strayed beyond justice and even-handedness. Perhaps, however, there is a mismatch between the values you espouse and those of your partner? This may seem irrelevant, but while the good manager will take care to keep the personal out of the work-place, the best managers are those who have their personal lives ordered and can take decisions from a position of emotional strength and security.

Increasingly, I find that the very best corporate managers and leaders are those who are emotionally robust and at ease with themselves. They may be eccentric or maverick but their self belief is very often underpinned by the belief of someone close to them, usually a partner. These days people marry increasingly late and it is rare for couples to form a contract (ahead of the birth of children at any rate) in which one focuses on their career and the other on the home. Very often the budding Chief Executive approaches the all-important middle phases of their career at the very point at which they seek to consolidate in their personal lives and settle down with a partner. It is important to find a match between the two aspects of life and to be comfortable that the person you are during the day is consistent with the one that you are when you return home. A few years into your career, then, it may be useful to return to the table in Chapter 1 and, based on some knowledge, see whether the attributes attached to business are still ones with which you are comfortable and against which you are comfortable to be judged.

A later educational choice

There is no perfect educational course which will prepare executives for a successful career. Indeed, the diagram on the next page demonstrates several ways in which you can make it with or without educational qualifications.

There are, however, ways in which people with some experience can consolidate that experience through more theoretical study. I refer, of course, to the much vaunted MBA. I have, in passing, referred to the MBA already as a mechanism to be used by people who may have missed out on tertiary education at an earlier stage. Classically, however, an MBA is something that appeals to two groups, either those wishing to make a career change or those wanting to further enhance their personal brand as a means of giving themselves access to accelerated progression.

In general I would not advocate that people study for an MBA until they have acquired some experience of work. Some business schools discourage applications from people with less than three years' work experience. The nature of most courses require some exposure to the problems which come under discussion. In my remarks here I want to focus on those people now in their late twenties or perhaps their early thirties who are on course, so far, to general management and who are considering the value of an MBA. In recent years business administration courses and, indeed, business schools have proliferated. The decision whether or not to study for an MBA

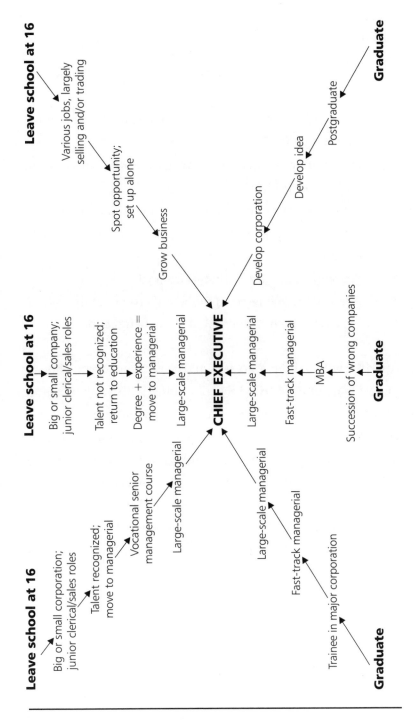

is becoming as fraught as earlier educational choices. In considering the question there are some very obvious issues to consider:

- Will an MBA materially add to your understanding of business?
- Does the sector in which you are engaged set store by such a qualification?
- Do you hope to gain better insight or to align yourself with better people?
- Is this a means of expanding your horizons, gaining exposure to people from different disciplines and different cultures?
- Are you trying to rehabilitate yourself?
- Are you more interested in the milk round at the end of the course than the period of study beforehand?

An MBA will take up a great deal of your time. If you choose to do a part-time MBA while continuing with your full-time job you may find that your performance in both suffers unless you have support from your employer, support at home and tremendous reserves of energy. If this is your chosen route you will need to be entirely committed. A full time MBA will be expensive and, unless you are sponsored by your employer, can be a heavy investment which will not necessarily generate as high a return as finding the right next job. Future employers will examine your motives in taking the MBA and will be cautious if your decision looks like an escape – no matter the personal sacrifices you may be making. The best situation in which to consider an MBA is from a position of strength. You are a high performer in your company. The company wishes to give you access to other high performers from different organizations and cultures. You need to be thrown back upon your own resources, put to different tests, forced to debate, learn, conquer areas of ignorance and, generally, be rounded, put in a position where you can reflect upon your own progress. In such circumstances an MBA can be invigorating, can enable you to measure yourself against the best of your generation and gain access to new ideas, insights into different business models, and a range of invaluable contacts amongst people of similar aptitude to yourself. In short, an MBA can be a means of rehabilitation but to rely on it being so is probably unwise. The qualification is most likely to give access to the giddy heights at the top of the corporation for those who are already on course to get there. It is, perhaps, more of a finishing school than a kindergarten.

Assuming you are one of those able and fortunate people who has found a niche in an appropriate organization there is every reason to continue to give prominence to branding when choosing a business school and a course. Strive for the best. Choose a school that speaks for itself on your CV, not one that you have to explain away. Have a strong rationale for your choice. Understand what a particular school can offer you. Where possible, throw yourself into the experience, maximize the opportunity and, much as you did at university, ensure that you explore life outside the class-room while also striving to make it to the Dean's list. An MBA should gild your CV – a bronze will not do. Go for gold. MBAs have become something of a distraction. They are only of value if they are valued. If you are successful and happy in a sector and corporation where there is no merit in taking time out, or possible disadvantage in removing yourself from the actuality of business life, do not do it.

As we reach the end of Chapter 2 we have reached the late twenties or early thirties in the life of our future Chief Executive. These have been turbulent years with difficult decisions and much learning about life, business and self. Above all they should have been questioning years with constant probing and evaluation and rigorous judgement exercised on one's values, skills and the environment in which these have been exercised. They should not have been lonely years. You should have amassed supportive colleagues and, importantly, wise mentors. You should have gained exposure to a range of challenging situations and should not have been comfortable at all times. You will probably have failed in some endeavours, but learnt by those failures, discovered areas of yourself where you need to improve and turned failure to your longer-term advantage. You will have learned one of the great tricks of success, to transform even weaknesses into strengths. This should give heart to those in whom the dream to be a Chief Executive is still very much alive but some of the opportunities are still missing. If you have managed to survive the early years of your career with the dream still intact then you are in with a fighting chance of realizing it. Indeed, I would expect you to be impatient now, chomping at the bit, desperate to take the next steps towards fulfilling your dream. What you have done so far has been important. What you do next, however, will be all-important.

CHAPTER 3

Snakes and ladders – the pitfalls for the would-be chief executive

Why so many with potential in their twenties lose their way in their thirties. Understanding the underlying structures and assumptions about business: oligarchy versus democracy. An authority index: how comfortable are you exercising or submitting to authority? Are you a frustrated entrepreneur, maverick, spoiler or corporate champion? Women in business – what is the truth about the glass ceiling and how can women break through it?

B ut just what do you do next? In many ways the bid by young hopefuls to be the Chief Executive of a listed company is not far removed from the bid by vast numbers of the population around the world to win the lottery once or twice a week. Many more people enter the race than can possibly win and, not infrequently, the winner of the race may appear to have been almost randomly chosen. Is there then, any point, in trying to fix the race for yourself? Can any amount of training or tactics really influence the outcome? My answer to this is a disappointingly equivocal one: yes and no. There are no guarantees of achieving the ultimate goal but there are steps to be taken that should, barring considerable misfortune or mistakes, take the aspiring Chief Executive as far as possible towards their dream. Want of either ability or stamina, bad luck, and simple accidents of board demographics or the quality of the competition may ultimately stand in the way of realizing that dream but, the consolation prize of having tried one's best is probably better than the imponderable, what if? It may be the case that you will only partially achieve your dream. Perhaps you will need to change sector to find your opportunity or settle for a business of more modest scale. Possibly you will find that your best means of realizing the dream is to go it alone. At this still quite early point in your career you should be focusing on consolidation of early success and acquiring the skills and amassing the experience which will make you into a rounded and tested contender for the role of Chief Executive in whichever field ultimately proves practical. This will be the terrain, however, of Chapter 4. In Chapter 3 I want to focus on the snares and minefields that can catch out the aspiring Chief Executive.

These, by which I mean your thirties, are dangerous times. I am struck by the fact that those who are corporate stars in their twenties very often fall by the wayside during their thirties. Those who end up coming to the fore in their forties, therefore, are very frequently not those we might have predicted fifteen years previously. There are any number of reasons why this might be. As discussed in the last chapter, some people will simply choose to occupy a comfortable slot which enables them to find fulfilment in several areas of life and not just in their career. Some will reach the peak of their ability and settle, less willingly, perhaps, for a less elevated position than their original dreams might have dictated. For others the factors behind failure (or to be fair, want of success) may be less clear-cut and may reside in the bewildering terrain of attitude and cast of mind.

It is very clearly the case that the factors which make one successful at twenty-five or twenty-eight are not necessarily those which make people successful ten years on. Part of this has to do with the way businesses are managed and with the sensitivities we have towards managing and being managed. First we should consider the manner in which a young manager works in his or her twenties. Those in professional services will be familiar with the concept of finders, minders and grinders. A well-worn phrase it has, like most hackneyed epithets, the merit of being a fairly apposite description. Those at the top in a professional services firm find the work, those in the middle mind it and make sure it is executed appropriately, and those at the bottom do the hard grind to produce the results, the analysis and model building. The structures in a corporation are a bit different – certainly at the top – but the middle and lower levels mind and grind in much the same way as their counterparts in service businesses. In short, a young executive is likely both to give and take instruction in accordance with a hierarchy he or she will have been engaged in from the moment they became aware of the world around them. It mirrors the family and educational set-up with a comforting familiarity.

The young executive tolerates that structure on the assumption that it will, before long, give way to a different one where he or she will have more authority and voice. The graduate trainee or junior executive will put up with the indignities of their position knowing that their moment will come just as the small tyrannies of childhood gave way to the licence of adulthood. Some however, misjudge the timing of that process and fundamentally misunderstand the structures and systems of authority which pertain in most corporations. The mistake is easily made. As adults we actively participate in the government of society by exercising our vote in the democratic system. Democracy is the prevailing system of political government amongst the most affluent, generally Western, states of the world. While it is easy to assume that democracy prevails across all forms of organization it is certainly not the system by which corporations are governed. Indeed, the closest form we can find in the corporate world to the democratic political model is that of the partnership where the profits are shared and each partner has one vote. This form of organization is becoming increasingly out-moded and a number of partnerships have turned themselves into corporations. Of course, companies use the vocabulary of democracy and strive to be inclusive, to empower, to consult, to build consensus, but any impression that corporations are democratic is illusory.

Most corporations are run as oligarchies, with a few at the top taking decisions on behalf of the many. In the case of founder led businesses the model is that of an autocracy. Indeed, the shift from autocracy to oligarchy is one that many successful companies fail to achieve, a situation that can lead to terminal decline. Most of us experience business as hierarchy, with clear chains of command passing from top to bottom and accountability passing in reverse. The systems by which corporations are governed may seem to have little bearing on the success or failure of those promising young executives making their way through the ranks. In my view, however, the effect can be quite profound, particularly where the executive may be emotionally predisposed towards the conditions of democracy and uncomfortable with the consequences of oligarchy. In these days of decentralization and empowered businesses we can be forgiven for thinking that democracy is creeping into the organization but, ultimately, authority and power reside in the boardroom and with the top tier of management. It would be interesting to consider why business has not adopted the democratic model but is probably a subject for another context. The role and structure of the board is reminiscent of the Boule which supported the assembly in the cradle of democracy itself, ancient Athens. The Boule was a small council of some fifty people (drawn by lots) who prepared the agenda for the assembly meetings and mapped out how those assemblies would proceed. Essentially, the Boule stage managed the assembly ensuring the maintenance of cohesive relations. The board serves a similar purpose. There is little enthusiasm in any boardroom for a vote and boards are concerned with approving decisions already made elsewhere in order to maintain the smooth running of the business. Oligarchy is a risky business because it depends on like-mindedness on the part of its members, but seems to be favoured by business because division impedes action and businesses require action to survive.

Realistically, below that top tier in any corporation, managers may have influence and their actions can affect positively or negatively the scope and success of the enterprise but they have limited actual power and voice. They must continue to take instruction. The model is not unlike that of the armed forces (on which, of course, it was based). Command and control models are deeply out of favour and most corporations are substantially more enlightened than to emasculate the workforce by wresting from it all sense of control. Still, the fact remains, that success in a corporation does require a degree of comfort with authority being acted upon one. Equally, with increasing seniority executives must be comfortable to stand in an authoritative position over others. In corporate life, there is no notion of equality. There is an understanding of justice, of merit and of fairness, but parity and equity are terms normally reserved for discussions about pay rather than status.

We are really straying back to the subject matter of my opening chapter – values. Some people may be very successful in the early years of their career when they are happy to follow instruction. Indeed, they may display considerable initiative and far exceed the instructions given and so more than meet expectations. They may enjoy pleasing the authority figure. They may, however, find it uncomfortable becoming that authority figure. Indeed, the young executive who seeks to please may lack self-esteem, needing to find his or her sense of self-worth in the worth others attach to them. Such people seldom become strong managers of people and good givers of instruction because they are too concerned to be liked and need to please. This is an emotional rather than an ideological issue, but ideology can play its part too. Some, finding themselves in a position of authority, are uncomfortable taking a decision without debate, without a vote and without due democratic process being observed. Such people want to take into account too many views and to cast about for an all-embracing, terminally elusive solution and in so doing become stymied by inaction and, ultimately, fail. Of course the best manager and decision maker is one who *is* able to build consensus and consult so making their decision on the basis of the best possible information. The pace of business and the speed at which decisions are required may, however, preclude such care and require a more crude process. Successful managers in business are those who are at ease taking big decisions on their own without, necessarily, having recourse to others.

As we move through our careers the end point of our aspirations may change. Someone who first dreamed of becoming a Marketing Director will graduate to wanting to become a Managing Director and then a Regional Managing Director and so on. Some will make their first general management role in their early thirties and will find that this is not the end of the journey towards power and authority, but merely a step along the way. It is a commonplace event to find dissension between the corporate centre and the Chief Executive of a division within the corporation. Indeed, the phrase 'robber baron' has been coined to describe the turf-protecting divisional man who displays signs of paranoia in relation to the encroaching centre which seeks to deny or limit his power. Here the Managing Director has failed to understand the system of oligarchy which prevails and is, perhaps, a natural autocrat. Like a renaissance monarch he will fiercely protect his own key people but sees no loyalty to a greater body than himself. Armed with a good idea, this person might do better as an entrepreneur.

One of the reasons why a number of those who show early promise fail to fulfil that promise far into their thirties is simply because they are emotionally or intellectually out of sympathy with the management systems in a corporation. It is not easy to instruct others and to find a balance between self-respect and respect for others. Similarly, it is not easy to subjugate one's own authority to a higher one. In our increasingly secularized society we have taken to worshipping individualism, and yet corporations require individuals to sublimate their immediate personal interests to the greater good of the corporate entity. Success in a corporate environment does not require slavish devotion to the organization, but it does require a respect for it and a belief in what it is and does. There is little scope in business for any ironic sense of one's self, for business takes itself rather more seriously than this. Increasingly, young business talent is drawn from some of the best brains the universities have schooled. I have begun to notice how some outstanding young talents from Europe's top universities, all of whom would once have devoted themselves to public service, now see power as more likely to come to them through commerce than government administration or even politics. In one case the executive is a published author, an accomplished musician and a prize winner at every stage of his academic career. He happens, also to be multilingual. In another, a Southern European aged a little over 30 stands just outside the top executive team of a major North European company. His energy, creativity, passion and intellect have all brought him rapidly to the notice of a fairly conservative organization. In both cases these outstanding young people spend their days focusing on the production, marketing and distribution of detergents. Neither see any incongruity in this but identify their own success with the institution. To some extent the corporate man or woman must subsume his or her identity within that of the organization. Some overly internalize the corporate culture and some cultures lend themselves to this more than others, hence those at Procter & Gamble (P&G) who identify with the culture to such an extent that they loose their own identities altogether have been dubbed 'proctoids'. P&G and other organizations such as McKinsey or IBM or General Electric (GE) are well-oiled machines, where the whole is the sum of its parts. Interdependence rather than individualism is a measure of corporate well-being and those who recognize this and accept the checks and balances the institution places on their own personality are corporate champions, in all senses of the phrase, and likely to go far.

I recently undertook some work with a university college, described to me by insiders as one of the last surviving communes in the world. The form of governance was rigorously democratic, one person–one vote and lengthy discussion took place on all matters from decisions about key appointments to decisions about the proposed colour of a new carpet. My host, observing my disbelief at the system, told me of his own reactions when he joined the board of a corporation. He was astonished to find that, far from every decision being discussed and voted upon as a matter of normality, an issue went to the vote only in extreme situations. Much of the time the business was conducted on the basis of the say-so of one expert, drawing on the accumulated expertise of those reporting through to him. There was little doubt in his mind that the corporate system was the more efficient of the two, but he knew it would never work in his own environment because the individuals were ultimately greater than the whole. He also felt a profound unease about the veracity of the information put forward in the corporate environment. My observation of the college system was that democracy concealed a lack of trust whereas in a corporation which functions well there are high levels of trust, built up by the interdependence between the managing and the managed and the recognition that while each supports the other one *is* more senior than another.

If you are already in your first general management role and are starting to chafe at the constraints upon you then perhaps you are more naturally someone who should run your own business? Perhaps you believe that your own ideas are best and find it hard to be patient while the corporate process unfolds in order to give your ideas proper consideration? You may feel fierce loyalty to and from your team and trust your own ability to lead people to successful outcomes. All that is holding you back is the structure of the world you are in. One's early thirties is not a bad time at which to start considering entrepreneurial activities. Too much later and your risk profile may have changed with your personal circumstances and, barring the kind of disaster which can launch people on their entrepreneurial careers such as redundancy, it may seem altogether safer to stay in the corporate fold. Too much earlier and you may lack credibility – although some of the most determined and successful entrepreneurs start on leaving school and are untroubled by self-doubt.

Between thirty and thirty-five, with a decade or more of work experience behind you and some understanding of the disciplines and processes essential in a business, you will present a better option to those to whom you turn for finance. You should also have a sense of your market and the niche you wish to occupy. Setting up on your own is a huge step, assuming you want to build a business of reasonable scale. You need to be clear that your motives in leaving behind the career to which you had initially dedicated yourself are genuine. Do you have the drive, ambition, energy, self confidence, vision to see this through? Do you have the blessing of your closest advisers? Can you galvanize others into action, recruit your first team, carry conviction with the bankers? Is the idea robust, the business plan watertight, can you tolerate the uncertainty of the first months and years and are you prepared to compromise your lifestyle in the short term for the sake of longer-term gain? A random set of questions these, but you cannot afford to answer any negatively.

It would be wrong to suggest that anyone who does not entirely conform to the corporate model should step away from it. Homogeneity is not a guarantor of success. On the contrary, some of the most successful people in business are those mavericks who can do things a little differently, think more creatively, see imaginative connections or innovative solutions that do not appear to their more conservative colleagues. Perhaps in chafing against the constraints upon you, you are expressing a certain frustration with the status quo which is not at all ill-placed. Some critics of a corporation offer their criticism from a position of profound respect for the organization and a desire to see it flourish. These are potential rejuvenators and should be spotted and nurtured and most definitely not mistaken for the spoiler, the person who resents authority and who assumes that the corporation is a big brother, glowering presence in their life, bringing nothing but ill-will. The rejuvenator is comfortable in his or her own skin and not troubled by the requirement to be an amenable part of something larger than they are. The spoiler wants to be taken notice of, taken seriously and has a compulsion to be seen as equal to the corporation and a neurotic fear of being proven smaller than it and, most particularly, of being beaten by it. Spoilers can enjoy some success in a corporation for some time. Drawn to business because of its size and the comfort of its structures not to mention the possibility of excellent rewards – these are essentially insecure people – they can take pleasure in outpacing their peers and accruing power. Often unscrupulous they will network behind the scenes, enjoying their spider-like ability to catch others in their webs while themselves passing through the organization by way of the connections they have spun. Some spoilers can make it close to the top or even right to the top, driven by their individualism, ego and the anti-heroic aura which can attach to the inveterate critic. An organization where a spoiler makes it to the top is likely to be one in an advanced state of decline, where the organization as a whole has proven smaller than the will of the single spoiler. He or she will have made it to the top by exposing the deficiencies in others and, not having great strengths or a battery of solutions, will rapidly be exposed and, in their own fall, will take the organization with them.

It may be all too easy to mistake the spoiler for the maverick and the other way about. The maverick/rejuvenator is someone who sees a problem and plots a course to its solution. The spoiler will focus, ad nauseam, on the problem and declare it insoluble. Both will appear questioning but while the questions of one are intended to build understanding the questions of the other are meant to undermine. The maverick/rejuvenator, unlike the spoiler, has a healthy respect for the corporation but that respect is tempered by a lively scepticism and a questioning mentality that accepts only so much and only on the basis of a reasonable logic. Mavericks or rejuvenators, are the lifeblood of an organization. They will find new ways of acting and thinking and through a combination of self-belief and fundamental belief in the enterprise will forge the new.

Future success in an organization can depend, then, on the attitude of an executive to authority and their comfort levels with exercising authority on others and having it exercised upon themselves. The above details the varying types which emerge in corporate teams. Some should re-evaluate their career options and seek an alternative path, as shown in the table on the following pages.

In my previous book, *Drive: Leadership in Business and Beyond*, I wrote at length about the strong correlation between success at the top of businesses and oddity. There is also something of a correlation between success at the top of businesses and, to use British terms, a background that is not particularly privileged. Those autodidacts, self-taught or self-propelling individuals who enter the corporate fold tend to go further than some of their initially more polished peers. If you are in

Attitudes to authority and chances for corporate success

Type	Distinguishing features	Attitude to authority	Best route to success
Appeaser/pleaser	High-quality work, always exceeds expectations. Identified as high potential at a young age. Enamoured of the organization, a naturally corporate person, but crushed by its weight.	Very comfortable with authority being exercised upon them. Very uncomfortable exercising authority on others.	(a) Set up as a self- employed worker, providing exemplary work to a small client/customer base charging premium rates for a premium service. (b) Move into a role at the corporate centre with a strong project focus, working close to power, taking instruction but not managing others.
Autocrat/frustrated entrepreneur	High energy and drive. Thrusting corporate style. Full of ideas but impatient of process. Much loved by his/her team, misunderstood by his/her peers and an irritant to his/her superiors. Fascinated by the corporation, sees self as equal to it.	Naturally in charge and comfortable exercising authority. Resistant to authority being exercised on him/her.	To capitalize on early success the talented natural autocrat should probably take the corporate training and run. They should channel their energies and ideas into setting up their own business and have a fair chance of building a medium-sized enterprise.
Spoiler	Early success because driven by a neurotic need to prove him or herself. Cynical, complaining, critical – politically astute. Hectoring and bullying style can be disguised by honeyed tones and charming demeanour. Not always easily recognized. Fearful of the corporation, resentful of its power.	Resentful of authority exercised upon him/herself. Absence of real self confidence makes them poor at exercising authority judiciously over others. Inclined to try and exercise power rather than authority.	Not necessarily without talent spoilers can be redeemed in the right environment. Naturally more likely to succeed in a setting where authority is very loose, such as a partnership. Better engaged in an activity where criticism is a strength, so some form of professional service. Should not lead or run an organization but might lead or run an account.

Maverick/ rejuvenator	Slightly the odd one out. Will not necessarily shine from the outset – asks too many questions and thinks a little too much. Over time will come to be recognized for the quality of suggestions and thought. A straight-forward colleague, an inspirational subordinate and leader, although inconsistency can undermine effectiveness. Intrigued and fascinated by the corporation.	At ease with the exercise of authority on himself and over others, but questioning of decisions within framework of overall acceptance.	Intrigued by large scale businesses and a believer in the corporation the maverick is best in this setting with good people around to spark and clearly defined norms within which he or she can differ and be creative. To fulfil potential mavericks need good mentors. Without them they will be lost in the undergrowth and will need to move on. With them, the sky's the limit. Mavericks are at their best where major change is needed.
Corporate champion	Effortlessly rise to the top in all they do. Talented, susceptible to being trained, independent of thought but cognizant of the interdependence of business. A natural élite in business.	Fully understand the rules of engagement. Comfortable being managed and managing. Know when to push and when to hold back.	High potential to go far in a corporation. Only things to steer them off course will be an unexpected change in business circumstances which brings the maverick to the fore. Good for stable times. Certainly strong contenders for board positions.

your early thirties currently you may be finding for the first time ever that you are truly standing on your own two feet. Up until now you have been propelled by the octane of parental ambition and the preparation they have put into ensuring that you have the necessary opportunities from which to achieve greatness. Curiously, despite all their efforts to the contrary, this preparation for life, carefully constructed by your parents and perhaps your teachers, can be your greatest disservice. Some of you may wake up to the fact that you have become so accustomed to life as the willing recipient of the care of those in authority that you have become, without meaning to, an appeaser/ pleaser. Others may simply find that the energy is wanting, the hunger and passion, the drive to take you onto the next phase. Perhaps you have gone further than your guides and mentors have gone. They cannot advise you any longer, now all is down to you. So unused are you to finding your own solutions that you stumble and fall. Perhaps the most dangerous effect of privilege is that it blunts one's sense of urgency or even renders the lucky recipient complacent. Everything has gone right for me so far, why should matters change? Equally, those who have spent a lifetime in comfortable middle-class surroundings, at good schools, in nice homes, excellent universities, blue-chip companies have limited experience of extremity. Those who have experienced profound difficulty at a young age have acquired strategies for dealing with extreme situations which can be invaluable later. As I proved with extensive examples in *Drive: Leadership in Business and Beyond*, those who have made it to the top in business are very often those who have experienced early hardship. The most common example is loss of a parent at a young age – which may confer a sense of responsibility on the bereaved child, making them want to live on behalf of the lost parent, giving them a sense of the gift of life they have been given and must use to the full and, accustoming them to loss and hardship which gives them a protective shell. Other examples of early hardship include loss of social status through sudden poverty, poor health impeding educational progress, a sense of alienation as an immigrant in the community. Look at the biographical data on the Chief Executives of Fortune 500 global companies and you will find a litany of distress, disappointment and misery, overcome through drive, determination and tenacity.

By now those of you reading this who come from a comfortable background, have both parents still living, and have lived with little serious pain or grief in your life may be on the point of rejecting this thesis altogether and discarding the book in frustration. Of course there are products of similar backgrounds to your own at the helm of major enterprises. I can think of several eminently sane characters with little scarring from life who have made it to the top with no evidence of oddity. I suspect, however, that put them in the psychiatrist's chair for a small amount of time and the inner demons would be revealed. If you are to make it to the top you will need to be obsessive, you must want this with passion and fervour. If you do not, then the passion and fervour of others who do will lead to your more moderate desires being swept aside.

I said at the outset of this chapter that a striking number of people who appeared destined for success in their twenties have disappeared from view by their thirties and forties. The most striking incidence of this is, of course, among women.

Much has been written on this subject by people better qualified than I. It does, however, merit mention and a few comments. First, there are some extremely obvious points to be made. In recent decades there has been a very strong trend towards women postponing having children until they have established themselves in a career. Typically, this means that they start their families in their thirties. At a crucial point when their male peers are consolidating and rounding out their skill sets women are absent from the workplace or situated in such a way that they cannot take on the next logical assignment owing to recent or impending pregnancy. Legislation exists to protect the rights and interests of women in this situation but no amount of legislation can compensate a woman for a missed opportunity. Nor can legislation protect against certain assumptions and prejudices. Once a woman has had one child it is not unreasonable to suppose that she may want another in relatively quick succession. She may not be presented with an opportunity simply because of an assumption, right or wrong on the part of her employer, that she will shortly be unavailable.

Despite a vast increase in paternal involvement in child care it is fair to say that ultimate accountability lies with the mother. Indeed, it is more socially acceptable for that to be the case. If a woman leaves a meeting early because of her commitments with children it may provoke irritation. When a man leaves a meeting early for the same reason it may provoke mirth and a lack of respect. Thus the requirement to be home on time to take over from the individual providing child care more often falls on the mother than on her partner. The upheaval of motherhood, the sleepless nights, the emotional chaos of the early months can take its toll and perhaps some women are less effective than when they were child-free. Many mothers of my acquaintance would quarrel with this view. Having less time to devote to more interests requires women to become particularly adept at time management and prioritizing. Motherhood, these women would say, can lead to more rather than less efficiency. This may be the reality but it is quite possibly not the perception. Moreover, motherhood – and parenthood in general – leads to a modification of one's world view and the new parent has a different perspective on life. With many women this can lead to greater sense of proportion and balance. Many might assume that this new sense of equilibrium squeezes out the priorities of the workplace. A passion for internal audit might diminish and a desire to be the next Finance Director seem less pressing when a baby is introduced into one's life and absorbs one's passions and interests. In my experience the newly acquired sense of balance can actually be much more positive and act to the advantage of the woman. Their new outlook on life can enable them to act with more assurance and confidence. Trivia seems just that. There is less time for distraction and women focus on what matters. Many women, in short, acquire more authority than they lose from motherhood.

There are, however, some unavoidable consequences of biology. Some women simply decide that they cannot balance a fast-track career with the provision of a suitable environment for their children. Amongst professional working couples of equal status and ability there is often an overt agreement that the male career will take precedence while the woman balances children and work. This decision reflects the belief that if both are obliged to compromise on behalf of the family, then both will miss out on career opportunities given to other people without conflicting priorities. That being so it seems sensible that only one of the two should sacrifice their career. The woman then will settle at a particular plateau. Indeed, for organizations this can be very important; to have very talented people settling to remain in middle management for positive reasons can provide stability and enduring quality of performance.

Many organizations have become much more flexible about working arrangements precisely to try and keep hold of the female talent in which they have invested. A senior woman of my acquaintance has had her right to work from home one day a week written into her contract. Another organization I know actively encourages people to work a four-day week (pro rata of course) on the basis that breadth in life will lead to better outputs (this is a professional services business). Technology has enabled much more flexibility and the numbers of women who are able to maintain a senior career alongside having a family can be expected to grow significantly over coming generations. There are substantial pay-offs for organizations who do offer support to their female executives with children. A primary one is the loyalty they can expect. Not infrequently my colleagues in executive search find that women are not prepared to consider moving until they feel they have 'paid back' their company for the support it has provided.

While biology certainly accounts for some of the women who are lost to the upper echelons of business, it does not account for all. While there is unquestionably chauvinism in all walks of life, I am not really prepared to believe that there is a whole-sale rejection of female talent by corporate bosses. Indeed, there are many corporate bosses of my acquaintance who would welcome having more women amongst the candidates for senior posts. The issue is not so much that women are being denied opportunities at senior levels as that they have fallen by the wayside long before having the opportunity to be selected for a board position. There is some cause for opti-mism. More women are being appointed to senior positions and in some very strong cultures where we might expect change to be slower. A 40 year old woman is President of Asia for Coca Cola, for instance and is the most senior woman in the business and the youngest ever President. Another Ameri-can woman hit the headlines when she became the Chief Financial Officer of Royal Dutch Shell. The appointment of Judy Boynton to this role represented a double first for the company: the first time they had appointed a woman to such a senior position and the first time they had gone outside the organization to appoint at this level. The newly appointed Dean of the London Business School is Laura Tyson – while it may be stretching the truth to claim this as a business appoint-ment it is not inaccurate to claim that this is a position of some influence in the business community. Intriguingly, Tyson is another successful American woman, as of course is the only woman running a FTSE 100 company, Marjorie Scardino. The prominence of *American* women in British business may be a mere accident but may also reflect the different attitudes towards business in Europe and the United States.

In an earlier book, *The Culture Wars*, I wrote extensively about European resistance to and the US valorization of business. The United States is, famously, the home of business, hence in launching an assault upon that nation, terrorists chose a potent symbol of business, the World Trade Centre, as their target. In Europe there is far greater ambivalence towards the profit principle and a belief that old money is better than new, with a lingering disdain for 'trade' and all its connotations. Instead, the professions are regarded as more respectable, and though this is changing, there is still a high degree of prejudice towards the commercial world and a low level of trust. Over the course of the twentieth century as women began to enter the workforce and to take on positions equivalent to their male contemporaries, we have seen many women be success-ful but (certainly in the UK and in Europe) more of them in the so-called 'caring professions' than in the strictly commercial world. Perhaps the advisers to young women have felt this milieu a more appropriate one in which a woman might exercise her skills? Women have made excellent teachers, headmistresses, doctors, nurses. Women have also been suc-cessful in public service, in the civil service, or as lawyers and barristers. Indeed, in institutions where the purpose is less easily reductive to one word (as in business that one word would be profit), women seem to have fared better. Better, but, arguably, still far short of their male counterparts. Interest-ingly, too, these environments have worked harder sooner to try and ensure that women have opportunities to excel and make it to the top. Companies are now very much aware of the glass ceiling which seems to intrude between women and ulti-mate success, but are relatively powerless to shift the balance so that men and women achieve in more equal numbers.

It is hard to embark on any discussion of this subject without appearing to rework old prejudices. All the same, there are some behavioural traits in women – no doubt conditioned – that we can establish as being more female than male. For instance, in the arena of soft skills there is little doubt that women are more intuitive than men, more aware of the social mix of which they are a part and more easily able to suspend ego in a group situation. Indeed, one vital role many women play in business is that of a senior secretary to directors. Time and again they prove themselves able to observe and understand the subterranean workings of a corporation and to impart this knowledge to their boss in such as way that their boss may believe the intelligence to be his own. Where the boss is female the relationship may still operate in a similar way, with the secretary able to be the eyes and ears of their boss who might simply not have the time, or indeed the access, to understand the issues which are important across the workforce. Perhaps the principal difference between the interaction between a secretary and a female boss is that on these issues, at least, there may be more of a dialogue.

Women are generally more socialized than men. Very possibly a conditioned response, it is nevertheless observable from a very young age. Little girls play in groups and play nurturing games. Little boys when they play in groups are more likely to be marauders than nurturers. This focus on caring is something society tacitly expects of women in their roles as daughters, wives and mothers and, indeed, secretaries. Women are encouraged to focus on their emotional lives, to express themselves openly and to share their feelings, to confide. Even in these highly liberated days, women who want children are compelled in part by the ticking of their biological clocks to focus on finding a partner. Once they have settled down in a loving and, to use the term again, liberated partnership the chances are that they will bear the burden of the greater part of the caring elements of the home. Men unquestionably do more than they did but women, equally unquestionably, do most. These platitudes may appear to have a whiff of sexism about them. My intent is to point out that women have a wide angle vision of the world whereas men are able to have a zoom vision This wide angle vision enables women to be creative, to have an excellent ability to synthesize material, to play a number of different roles successfully at any one time, to be multi-tasked and to parallel process with flair and efficiency. Small wonder that women are very often outstanding in a professional services environment (although the numbers of women directors in McKinsey, Bain and Booz Allen scarcely bear this out). In terms of inclination, women are perhaps less drawn to environments with a narrow or single focus. It is, as we have seen, possible to reduce the rationale behind business to a single word – profit. It is hard to do the same for the public and voluntary sectors which allow satisfaction of a number of different areas and are multi-purpose. A little earlier in this chapter I described two outstandingly able men who have committed themselves to the fortunes of detergents – real evidence of a zoom focus. For women, no matter how capable they are of focusing on a given task, such an obsessive focus on something so apparently trivial, can be anathema.

I have met plenty of arrogant women but I still have little hesitation in stating that I find men in general to be more egotistical and more driven by ego than most women. Certainly men are more given to vanity than women. This may well have its roots in the tendency among women to see themselves in relation to others and to give greater quarter to others as a result. The reckless self-assurance of the young man, sometimes founded on nothing of any substance and seldom diminished by exposure to others more worthy than himself, is rarely to be found in a young woman of the same age. A 25-year-old woman is very often much more considered and intelligent in her judgements and pronouncements than a 25-year-old man but the male ego which can make a young man insufferable is also a useful tool that can make him more successful in the long-run. Self-belief, hopefully well-founded, provides the confidence from which to succeed in business. Business requires self-belief. So, you might say, do other walks of life. The barrister, the headmistress, the paediatrician all require self-confidence and self-belief in order to be credible with the populations they address. In these instances, however, the role itself engenders a form of confidence. Business denies women a clear-cut role and without a clear role to fall back on, women require self supporting self confidence.

Business, equally certainly, denies women a clear-cut uniform. The barrister can wear her wig and robes, the doctor her white coat and even the headmistress has a uniform of a kind, smart but sensible rather than glamorous. The woman in business must struggle to capture the right tone in her appearance and, of course, her appearance will matter. There can be no escaping the tyranny of our universal obsession with female appearance. Take Cherie Blair or Hilary Clinton – independently successful women in their own right, both, once they became consort to men in powerful positions, became subject to extensive and negative commentary on their appearance, so much so that they were obliged to take professional advice on the subject.

Men in business can, by and large, get away with a very straightforward dress code – a suit, shirt and tie in the UK and US and slacks and casual jacket in Europe. Many are the men who have sighed a sigh of relief with the decline of dress-down days as commerce recovers from the dot-com craze and its associated follies. The hapless, fashion-ignorant male can retreat into the safety of his navy blue suit with his only delicate decision being whether to consign his Mickey Mouse tie to the bottom drawer or not. Not so women in business, for women must suffer the equivalent of dress-down day every day. Some get it right, others do not, but getting it right or wrong is an art – the right length of skirt, height of heel or depth of neckline, the colour and style of hair, the right amount of make-up, an appropriate scent, discreet jewellery, the quality of the fabric, the cut. A fraction of every woman's day must be spent making important decisions on these minutiae. Of course it should not matter what a woman looks like and her appearance should not be a matter of comment, any more than should a man's. We all know, however, that irrespective of a woman's role, her appearance will come into question and there is an entire vocabulary to describe the woman who somehow does not strike the right note. All that this amounts to is that women have to clear certain hurdles that are not even put in the path of men if they are to be taken seriously.

Business does have some odd obsessions about male appearance. Perhaps the most common of these concerns beards, which have been widely frowned upon in the past and which remain deeply unfashionable in most boardrooms. Pondering why this might be, I conclude that part of the aim of any business person is to look fairly anonymous so as not to detract from the product or service they are concerned to promote. The IBM and McKinsey uniform of the very white shirt, and the navy blue suit, derives from precisely this philosophy. In business there is no call for overt individualism, rather a strong sense of cohesion in the corporation – evidence once again that business calls for the sublimation of self to the bigger idea of the company or commercial endeavour. Perhaps there is a message for women in this; that in their style of dress they should seek very definitely not to stand out. They will have succeeded if their colleagues, clients or customers recall them to be well-groomed and smart without recalling any outfit in particular!

The structures of business, aping those of the military services, were established by and for men. The banter and easy camaraderie that can be observed amongst men in an office is not a particularly natural atmosphere for women to partake of. Some of the team-building acts that businesses engage in, a round of golf, a drink in the pub or even more formalized shoots or sporting events, tend to appeal more to men than to women. Some women, uncomfortable in these situations or simply unable to attend due to domestic obligations, find themselves excluded from a forum which, explicitly social, implicitly ends up being one where decisions may be considered and very often made. Business really does not encourage intimacy or emotion but favours a light touch and a phlegmatic approach to life. At the risk of making sweeping generalizations, women as they grow up tend to engage in close friendships with a small number of friends to whom they confide everything. Entering the business world, women must change gear from this type of friendship into a much more fluid and loose set of relationships. Perhaps I am selling business short in saying this, but business is superficial in some regards and is ill-disposed towards intensity. It is very often important to understand the psychology between a buyer and a seller, to recognize market place trends and to extrapolate from certain sets of behaviours that others will follow but seldom is one required to make deep and penetrating assessments of others. Relationships, stemming as they do from individual needs and concerns, are again generally sublimated to the broader corporate entity. Women must adapt to an environment that is very likely to offer significant intellectual stimulation in other ways and will call upon a very broad range of skills but will favour thinking over feeling. It is interesting to note that women have been successful entering the accounting profession and then moving into corporations as the Chief Financial Officer. The CFO who sits at the centre of a business and must be highly analytical, well-informed, impartial and objective is not a bad paradigm for a corporate business-person, the closest we come to finding a clear-cut role.

So, if you are a very talented woman in your early thirties can you take control of your destiny in this world which appears structured to exclude you or to banish you to the sidelines? Are there any guidelines you can follow? I think there are, although they may require women to sacrifice principles they hold dear.

- Cultivate a reputation for excellence and exemplary performance. As you move through the corporate hierarchy make sure you favour those who are top performers, irrespective of gender.

- Maintain your own counsel; do not turn to others for advice or offer confidences but maintain a friendly and helpful distance;

- Do not make an issue of your gender. On occasion, especially when goaded, this may be difficult but you should be more interested in championing your own career than a cause, however just and important.

- Ensure that you are well-groomed and well-dressed but do not stand out.

- Do not use manipulative behaviour that may be deemed 'sexual wiles' – don't play into the hands of any would-be detractor.

- Favour analytical rigour over emotional accuracy; beat your male colleagues at their own game.

- Convert analytical rigour into emotional accuracy. Deploy your superior intuitive skills in a manner that neither undermines nor threatens but is professional and useful, i.e. in well-honed judgements concisely expressed and delivered at the right moment.

- Be prepared that you will have to work harder to achieve the same amount as your male colleagues since you will, inevitably, encounter some prejudice.

- Recognize that you do have champions and that our corporations need you. Look for your support and use it.

- Don't be afraid of taking advantage of any positive discrimination. Seize your opportunities when they present themselves.

This may read like an offensive litany of self-repression and you may feel that too much sublimation of self is required for success, particularly if you relish the wide-angle vision which does seem to be one of the properties of the female gender. One simple reason why many women do not reach the top may be that they have too much sanity and lack the overriding obsessive desire to be kingpin. For those who do, but do not want to succeed at the cost of their self-image then maybe the best choice is to set up on their own. Women make very successful entrepreneurs or lone operators. Their stamina, wide-angle vision of the world, perfectionism and flexibility can go a long way to compensate for generally lower tolerance for risk.

In your twenties and thirties you will be climbing a number of career ladders, but you may slide down any number of snakes. It is my contention in this chapter that many of these will be to do with your appetite for the corporate entity and your willingness to make substantial sacrifices in order to fit in. Understanding where you come on any authority index and measuring your ability to suppress your personality to the benefit of the corporation will help make sure that the snakes you slide down will be the short ones with a ladder just a throw of the dice away. Business may be superficial in some ways but it has a shallow but endearing obsession with success. Most corporations set out to make their employees successful and increasingly offer tangible rewards for closely measured success. With the will of the corporation on your side coupled with genuine talent and real insight into your self, you have a very good chance of winning this particular board game.

CHAPTER 4

A monopoly on talent? The years of consolidation

Career consolidation. Understanding the process by which a Chief Executive is appointed and what the decision makers will be looking for. How to accumulate the right experience, which risks to take, how to put yourself to the test. The 6 Cs of success. What to do and what not to do in your thirties and forties.

I f we stick with the metaphor of board games, then Monopoly® provides an excellent motif for this chapter, which will consider how aspiring Chief Executives should build on the foundations of their early career in order to give themselves an excellent chance of being selected to lead a company. Naturally, this is still a game of chance and you are as dependent as ever on the roll of the dice. All the same, there is a clear strategy that will enable you to win. Buy up everything, but don't just do the obvious thing and save all your efforts (and cash) so that you can put your hotels onto Mayfair. Invest on your apparently weaker fronts, put a hotel or two on the

Old Kent Road. Provide yourself with ballast and surprise your opponents so that when they move around the board you are always there, strong and well-covered, from Vine Street to Piccadilly Circus.

Perhaps the biggest mistake an aspiring Chief Executive can make at this point in his/her career is to focus only on strengths. Up until now the primary concern of all our aspirants has been to demonstrate excellence. In order to achieve a sufficient platform from which to launch your senior career you have focused all your efforts on ensuring that you have areas of expertise which are universally acknowledged. You may have a particular reputation for relationship management or technical prowess of which you are justly proud. But just as it is pointless to put 25 hotels on Mayfair to the exclusion of all other properties if no one ever lands on it, so it is pointless to continue to hone your primary skills. That is the route to limitation not extension. Now is the time to broaden and to act, to add genuine achievements to the universal perception of talent. As Chief Executive you will encounter a vast array of different scenarios. You cannot predict at this point in your career what point in the business cycle will have been reached when you finally take on the top job. Nor will you know what the competition will look like, particularly if you are in a rapidly consolidating world. Perhaps technologies will have changed dramatically or new markets suddenly opened up or familiar ones, for whatever reason, closed down. As Chief Executive you need to have breadth of experience and a range of skills to help you in any eventuality. Importantly, as you reach your thirties you are probably still someone who is high potential rather than a proven top performer. Your thirties must be about realizing and proving that potential. Henry Ford offers an insight which every high potential executive should keep by them like a talisman: 'You cannot build a reputation on what you are going to do.' You have built expectation, now you need to secure a reputation.

It is probably worth fast-forwarding for a moment to consider the process by which a Chief Executive is likely to be appointed in a listed company. In general a nomination committee will be appointed. That committee will comprise the Chairman and a couple of the Non-Executive Directors. It should not ideally (although occasionally it might) include the outgoing Chief Executive. The committee is increasingly likely to seek outside advice on the appointment from a search (or headhunting) firm. If you are one of the potential internal candidates you might feel threatened by the prospect of an external search and infer from this decision that there is something wanting amongst the internal candidates. You should not be alarmed or draw any particular inference from this circumstance. Today boards are clear that they have a mandate to look after shareholder interests and the choice of Chief Executive is one of the most obvious opportunities they have of so doing. A board can consider that it has done well by its shareholders if it evaluates the very best internal candidates against the best external candidates. If then the internal appointment is appointed both the board and the candidate, not to mention the shareholders, know that the choice has been put to the test and validated by the market. There can be no better footing on which to commence a Chief Executive career. One final sophistication will come when it is better understood on the outside that the search process is giving way to a much broader consultative process. Increasingly we, the search community, find ourselves being involved in helping to define and articulate the requirements for the appointment. While we do, of course, use our knowledge of the external market to identify and bring forward the best of the talent outside an organization we have no vested interest in seeing one of the external candidates being placed. Indeed, we are likely to be involved in evaluating all candidates and will make our assessments and recommendations based on the best fit against the originally defined parameters. I am working, at the time of writing, on one situation where it is very possible that there will be no external search but where our skills will be used evaluating a broad internal field of applicants. Our knowledge of external benchmarks will be useful in this instance, but in providing a context rather than competition.

I have dwelt on this point not because it is a particular professional hobby-horse of my own, but because understanding the role of the search firm may be critical to you. It may be the case that you have no intention of looking outside your particular business and you may assume, therefore, that you need not take a headhunting call. In fact, a good headhunter could well be a very useful partner in your career, able to coach and advise and offer invaluable insights into the world of other companies and other executives of which you inevitably have only limited knowledge. While you may cherish the ambition (and have a good chance of realizing it) to be the Chief Executive in the company where you have spent your entire career to date, you may find it helpful to gain experience of board practice by being a Non Executive of another company. Indeed, some boards welcome the presence of an 'up-and-coming' executive on the board and many companies are prepared to release high potential executives for the necessary day or so a month to participate in what can be invaluable developmental experience. Headhunters are very often the means by which you can secure one of these coveted appointments.

My purpose in moving forward to consider the nomination process of Chief Executives was to focus on the fears and wishes of those making the final selection. I am struck by the line of questioning that the nomination committee will pursue with me when we discuss potential candidates. It is assumed that, since the candidate is being mentioned in this context, he or she has the requisite strengths. The nomination committee will be interested to understand where the balance of those strengths lies and may discard some candidates because their particular strengths are not consistent with the immediate needs of the business. Most important, however, and where members of the committee will focus their probing, will be on the area of weaknesses. Assuming this to be a well-chaired Nominations Committee, then it is not uncommon to find that the group will return again and again to this point until they are satisfied and convinced one way or another as to the precise risk as well as the precise opportunity that a given candidate represents. You may be outstanding in five out of six key areas, but if you are dangerously weak in the sixth you are unlikely to carry the day. While the best nominations committees are those who have the courage to take something of a risk (like Sir Patrick Gillam as Chairman of Asda appointing Archie Norman), no self-respecting committee should consider appointing a candidate about whom there is too great a risk. Such a decision would represent a significant dereliction of duty.

I am not suggesting that you should aim to eradicate all weaknesses. This would be both an impossible and, I am tempted to suggest, undesirable task. Weakness provides humanity and will also enable you to surround yourself with others whose talents offer an interesting complement to your own. In the previous chapter I have discussed the extent to which the corporate entity takes precedence over the individual. Increasingly management literature focuses on the extent to which no major corporation is led by one individual but by a group which the one individual, the leader, brings and binds together. During your thirties you should try to address weaknesses (if not entirely erase them) that will really impinge on your ultimate success and in so doing you will come to understand the reality of your weaknesses. In this way when you are asked to describe your weaknesses at a crucial point in the process – perhaps by the nomination committee – you will not fall back on the stock 'I don't suffer fools gladly.' Instead, you should aim to give a cogent analysis of the real weaknesses, what you have done to erase them and how you think you might compensate for them once in situ. And, by the way, the line 'I don't suffer fools gladly' is a betrayal of misjudgement in itself. Businesses comprise many different talents and part of being a successful manager is being able to make much of a little, to find the reservoir of talent even amongst the most unpromising team.

The Nomination Committee will be looking for skills. Skills, however, are meaningless unless they are put to the test. It is possible that I am a gifted artist but, never having taken up a paint brush I cannot know. Do not make the mistake of resting on your laurels only to find, too late, that the skills you have assumed are yours are not merely latent but non-existent. You should now be aiming to put the skills you believe you have firmly to the test. Let us assume, then, that you are on the brink of your first major appointment – as, if you are on track, should be the case. You should not, at this point, find yourself in a position of lonely isolation trying to evaluate what it is best to do next. If you are regarded as high-potential the organization for which you work will probably be as keen to nurture you as you are to be nurtured. A good organization will study the precise career opportunities that you need in order to become a fully rounded, balanced General Manager – the objective of this period. Life may be a little lonelier if you are the maverick described in the earlier chapter. Quite possibly you are still seen as a minor irritant in some quarters and need a more generous helping of luck than your colleagues who are in the mould of corporate champions. To a certain extent, you can make your own luck. Investigate where there have been other mavericks in the business, try and bring yourself to their attention. It is far from inconceivable that the person heading the organization at present is just such a maverick and may recognize a similar spirit in you. Perhaps you need to move into the centre to be seen for the constructive corporate critic you really are, to have your ideas seen in the spirit from which they come rather than as mildly seditious. Manoeuvre yourself into the right situation to gain the levels of recognition which will then bring the corporation to your aid over this all-important decade. Longfellow offers another important epithet: 'We judge ourselves on what we feel capable of doing. Others judge us by what we have already done.' For the maverick it may be harder to find the right outlet for potential.

One of the first things you should aim to do is to risk yourself. The younger you can acclimatize yourself to risk, the easier you will find it in future to adapt and find resources to cope with a challenging situation. Just as you would introduce a small child to water very early to encourage them to become a strong swimmer, so you should leave behind the safe harbour of the known environment as soon as possible if you are to prove a flexible executive and one for all seasons. There is, of course, a small risk that early acclimatization to risk can lead to recklessness; I am talking about measured risks here, those which you can measure and quantify by a mix of logic and intuition (or applied experience). One of the biggest risks you can take is to leave the safety of the organization that has sponsored you and move overseas. To the British and Americans, with our outrageously poor language skills, this represents a major act of personal exposure: although in many cases the local operating language will be English, nevertheless life outside work will require you to diversify and develop new skills. This suggestion presupposes that you are in a corporation which has multiple operations around the globe. This may not be the case, in which case you should seek to identify situations which conform broadly to the following:

- A different culture prevails from the one you have been used to.
- You are not known by your peers and superiors and cannot rest on any reputation.
- You have a specific task to achieve, so that your success or failure can be measured.
- You are operating in some area of the unknown – be it in a new language, a new business area or perhaps a new function.

The new pioneering you needs to guard against some obvious pitfalls:

- Is your destination important in the group? In terms of profits, size, strategy?
- Will you be acquiring skills and experiences which can be applied elsewhere in the business?
- Will you remain visible?
- Is the task assigned to you a realistic and viable one or could you find yourself scapegoated for the failure of someone else?
- Is the task sufficiently challenging? Will you really be markedly expanding your skill-set or putting it to difficult tests?

It is particularly important to position yourself in such a way that you are given assignments with a very clear mandate where you can amass significant and measurable achievements. It is no bad thing to evaluate each new role as a headhunter might.

- What are the dimensions of this business: size, profits, margins, employees, market share?
- Where does this put me in the overall company: in the biggest division, in the division regarded as most dynamic, in a tired, non-core division that is a target for disposal, in a tired division but one with latent potential needing to be fixed?
- What can I achieve: an improvement in profits; a turn-around; an improvement in quality leading to improved revenues and market share; improved morale of people leading to overall improvements in performance and

revenues; dramatically reduced costs; major streamlining of processes; major new installation of technology or production equipment?

- Who will I learn from? Where will I find my mentors?

You need to feel confident that there is a strong rationale behind your acceptance of this appointment. Imagine you are resigning from the company to take up this appointment elsewhere – how would your decision be received? Look at an opportunity from a range of angles but remain mindful that whatever decision you take now will have an enormous impact on your personal brand, to return to the theme of our first chapter. Go through the mental exercise of putting this on your CV. Does it enhance, is it out of kilter with the general trend of your CV? Does it require explanation but, in the light of that explanation, appear credible? A headhunter will look to see that you are clearly on a forward trajectory and that you have been able to take the company from one point to another, enhanced point. They will also look to see that you have amassed the following general experiences:

- Managing people of mixed ability.
- Building and motivating teams.
- Recruiting, developing and retaining first-class people.
- Identifying and grooming a successor.
- Developing a profile in the market, perhaps participating in industry fora.

Perhaps the role that you have been offered does not offer you the chance to have a demonstrable impact and to make a real difference. It might be the case that you have been offered a plum job in a major division where the general attitude, rightly, is that of 'if it ain't broke, don't fix it'. If this is the case, well done. You will be facing challenges of a different sort. You may find that you are following in the wake of one of the company's biggest young stars, giving you a very hard act to follow. Yours may be the division that is seen as a barometer of company performance, in which case your attention to detail needs to be absolute and your husbandry second to none. This careful management of the status quo in the face of shareholder scrutiny and under the watchful gaze of the organization's talent scouts can be every bit as demanding as a turnaround of a smallish business somewhat at a remove from the day-to-day operations at head office.

Are you, perhaps, one of the mavericks in the business? Is the role you have been offered one of reasonable size and scope but in a business that is far-removed either in geography or activities from the core markets and products in the group? You will need to look very closely at the opportunity indeed and, in so far as you are able, complete your own *strengths–weakness–opportunity–threat* (SWOT) analysis. It may be the case that there is a real opportunity to develop this operation and that, in being put into the role, the corporation is testing your mettle and seeing whether in fact you are the maverick they suspect or simply the spoiler. If the business looks irredeemable to you it may be that your true worth remains unsuspected and you have been marginalized, put on the shelf. If that is the case then you probably need to look outside the business.

You should not be unduly alarmed if you cannot identify great people from whom you will learn in your immediate locale. It will be important for you to hang on to the mentors you have already acquired and you need to find a means of keeping open the communication between yourself and senior people who you rate and who rate you. Indeed, if you can amass genuine achievements you can call upon those senior figures to come and inspect the improvements you have made. But part of the test here is to see how well you survive without someone to guide and steer you. How well have you learnt by their example, can you put their tenets into practice when left to your own devices?

The six Cs of success

Various elements of your personality and emotional psyche should be tested by this important role:

- *Courage* – can you survive alone? Do you have the courage of your convictions?
- *Certitude* – how easily can you come to a decision?
- *Consistency* – are you someone who conveys that sense of certitude (but not inflexibility) such that others are confident in following you?
- *Confidence* – are you sufficiently confident in your own abilities to recruit people to your team who may be more able in some areas than you are yourself?
- *Clarity* – do you have a clear vision for the future of the business, that you can articulate with conviction?
- *Calm* –can you cope in a crisis?

This period may prove to be an intensely illuminating one. Often we cherish thoughts about ourselves out of habit. You may, for example, think you are a very gregarious character who needs the buzz of people around you. Sent away from family and friends you may discover tremendous reserves and resources and discover that a degree of isolation and strangeness can be liberating. Alternatively, you may make discoveries about yourself which are not as pleasing. Perhaps you have always seen yourself as someone others will follow (maybe you were a prefect, a captain of a sports team) but, for the first time, you find that others do not naturally follow you and that you have difficulty engaging with people. Maybe you have played a role very well, but is it you? Could you have played other roles just as well. Have you a high degree of flexibility. Maybe there is a parallel you. An even better one. Maybe that is why you don't always fit – or are perceived as a bit of a loose cannon. Perhaps you find your natural style is dogmatic or didactic? There are endless permutations. It is unlikely, however, that you will survive this experience without uncovering some surprising strengths and weaknesses. The trick is to use the knowledge to move yourself forward. Admit the weakness you have found and try and find a way of strengthening it. One simple way may be to hire someone who excels in the area where you are weakest. Observe how it is they achieve what eludes you? Can you learn from them?

Until this point in your life you have probably done most of your learning from those above you in a hierarchy. If you are managing a business you no longer have someone day-to-day overseeing your actions from whom you can learn as directly as once you would have done. Learning, however, is a process that is not dependent upon hierarchy. You may hold titular authority over some individuals who may leave you behind in some key skill areas. Naturally, if you are a general manager who has come to your present position from a background in finance you will have no hesitation in turning to people with an alternative expertise and asking for their advice and assistance. None of us have many qualms in admitting an experience shortfall. Where we all start to feel uncomfortable is in the skills arena. Where there is less obvious excuse for the absence of a particular skill (other than the overriding fact that you are human), admission of weakness can be quite threatening, particularly in the face of a colleague who is junior to you but clearly a rising star. Being a strong general manager is not about being either Superman or Superwoman. It is about being practical, pragmatic and using the resources available to you to maximize the opportunities for the business and minimize its threats. Sensible use of human resources without any regard to ego will gain you notice and respect in a way that any solipsistic seeking after personal perfection will not.

It is very likely that if you are in a large corporation or a company with enlightened human resource policies that you will experience 360° appraisal. You will be long accustomed to hearing what those above you in the hierarchy think of you. It may be disconcerting to see how you are perceived by your subordinates. If you naturally believe in the authority of the person above you it may be the case that you assume your own superiority to those below you. We are all familiar with the personality type who ingratiates him or herself with the senior team while being disdainful and careless or arrogant towards juniors. Understanding how you are perceived from a range of different angles can be enormously helpful. Where there is no institutional mechanism for collecting this information you could benefit from establishing an informal forum for bottom-up appraisal. Quite apart from what you may learn you will send a clear message that you welcome openness and are willing to listen. If your efforts to allow constructive criticism meet with a wall of silence then perhaps there is insufficient trust from your staff towards you to enable the openness you seek. You need to be fearless at this stage and to confront your demons, taking every opportunity to bring them to notice.

There are no hard and fast rules about what you should achieve by which time for the would-be Chief Executive. Realistically, however, you need to maintain an accelerated rate of progress if you are to become a serious contender for the top job in a corporation of any size and scale. Since there will be other contenders running alongside you, there is little chance for a spot of rest and recuperation along the way. Having secured and been successful in this key job you need to propel yourself forward, acquiring new experiences and honing your skills and shoring up your weaknesses. In my experience as a search consultant there are two key issues which candidates repeatedly fall down on: scale and level. Your ambition in practical terms should be to ensure that you manage increasingly large-scale concerns and raise your game to the most senior level possible. Naturally, that means get as far as you can as fast as you can – but it also means more than that. Raising the level of your game is about ensuring that you demonstrate stature and show the credentials to be expected of a genuine business leader. Project an image of yourself which looks forward to where you want to be, rather than looking back at whence you came.

To be more specific about the experiences and skills you should acquire during your early thirties and early forties it might be useful to revert to the generic skills and experiences that the all-important nomination committee will be seeking to find when they come to consider the shortlist for the Chief Executive of their corporation. I propose to look at experience first. Naturally, each organization will require certain sets of experience specific to their activities. Some companies will be better able to be flexible with regard to the experience profile than others. For all listed companies, however, there will be certain areas of expertise or exposure which will be required of their candidates for Chief Executive.

Financial acumen

The first (and there is no order of merit here) is an understanding of the financial markets. If you are a top performer it is unlikely that you will have reached this point without having made it your business to understand how the commercial world operates. Indeed, I would expect you to have a clear fascination with the structures of business and the methods by which businesses finance themselves. In short, you should have a fairly robust understanding of the financial markets, of financial instruments and something of the legal requirements underpinning companies certainly in your local market. It helps to have good accounting knowledge, to know your way round how a business works through numbers.

As Chief Executive you will be strongly identified with the organization you lead. You should exercise similar scrutiny on the organization as you have exercised on your own person *en route* to the top. You will need to see the company through the eyes of the financial community. It follows, therefore, that you should be entirely robust where the numbers are concerned. You may be a brilliant leader of people, a source of creative ideas and an inspiration to others but if you cannot predict with accuracy the financial performance of the company and be robust under questioning from analysts and institutional investors then you will never have credibility at the top of a business. If you are uncomfortable with the extent of your knowledge/experience now is the time to address the issue. You can:

- Take a course at a recognized business school which will hone your understanding – a corporate finance course for non financial managers.
- Engineer a move to a business which is active in mergers and acquisitions where you will necessarily become more involved on a day-to-day basis with financial engineering.
- Ensure that you have first-class finance people in your team. Make it your business to learn from them.
- Invoke the assistance of your HR support – see if they can find a project that will require you to gain some genuine exposure at this level. Enlist the support of mentors.

If you are on a shortlist with one other candidate and all things are equal between you save that the other candidate is known in the financial community and you are not, then that candidate will in all probability have the edge over you. Otherwise, while it is desirable that you be known and respected in the financial community the reality will be that until you have attained either the position of Chief Financial Officer/Finance Director or Chief Executive you will be unlikely to have a serious and strong reputation with bankers. In the absence of such a reputation you need to ensure that you are associated with successful companies such that when the Nominations Committee try and predict the reaction of the analysts who will scrutinize the committee's decision, they will see no obvious negative. Instead they should find positive evidence that the companies of which you have been a part have been financially sound and delivering value.

Managing change

As Chief Executive of a listed company you can guarantee some form of volatility. You may be lucky and find that you preside over a successful period of calm and trouble-free trading but I can scarcely think of any in recent times who have. And, even if you are so blessed, you will not be selected to experience this happy halcyon period unless the Nominations Committee feels confident that you are equipped to deal with the requirement for change should it arise. Nominations Committees have an uncanny knack of wanting to be prepared for all and every eventuality. In reality this means they will be looking for:

- Speed of response
- A degree of prescience, an ability to spot trends
- A preparedness to share with the Board concerns about imminent threats (of any kind) which may require significant change within the company
- Breadth of experience

- The ability to lead a major project and to ensure that there are processes in place which will enable implementation.

Above all, perhaps, the Nominations Committee will be looking for evidence of leadership. If you say 'change' will people react and follow? Do you have the understanding of your team such that you can redeploy people in the appropriate ways to ensure that change is effected? Do you have the judgement to spot which elements of your present activities can be preserved and which should go. Can you exercise similar judgement on the people in the business. Do you have the humanity to ensure that the necessary changes which may have very real consequences on people throughout the organization, are effected with tact, sensitivity, candour and appropriate speed? Do you have the strength of purpose to take difficult decisions and stand by them?

The best way of being able to answer these questions is by having put yourself to the test. It is hard to think of a career in which you will not have had to manage change. In recent times, with the very rapid changes in technology, global markets and a cycle of boom and bust, few people will have operated without significant experience of change. The issue here is that of scale. In this period of your career you should position yourself to ensure that you do have experience of a major integration exercise, or systems implementation, perhaps an entire rebranding and relaunch of a business – a period of change where the change has a decisive and positive effect on the business. Ideally you should aim to have experience of cross-disciplinary change where you will be dealing with an array of people, issues and processes that may be new to you as well as some which are familiar.

In managing your own career this is one of the areas where you may need to take an apparently backward step – or sideways move – in order to move forward. You should not turn down the opportunity to participate in a major change programme even if you would prefer an alternative option of running something (it's back to making sure that you are covered on all sides of the board: Trafalgar Square, Oxford Street, Pentonville Road, as well as the classier Mayfair). You will have other opportunities to run things, and better opportunities if you prove your worth as an agent of change in a project of importance to the Board (and it must be something that genuinely matters). Naturally, of course, you will need to be confident that you fully subscribe to the rationale underpinning the changes. Change for change's sake is folly and, where you encounter it, you will find a business that is poorly led.

There is risk involved in this strategy. Some visionary business people make changes which are ill-received, however right they may be. They fall from grace and few, if any, are reinstated – certainly not in the rather unforgiving British climate. If you are associated with change of this kind, then your fortunes may suffer too. However, this is the element of contingency (a major part in the success or failure of a Chief Executive) about which you can do nothing. Making it is as much about luck as it is about tactics.

Team-building and motivation of people

Here the Nominations Committee will not simply be looking for experience. Its members will be looking for evidence of excellence in team building and people motivation. The areas of experience which you should aim to build include:

- Building and motivating mixed-ability teams.
- Re-energizing demotivated staff, getting the best out of people.
- Building and managing multicultural teams.
- Building, managing and sustaining teams. Low turn-over rates and the subsequent success of key team members will be an important measure of success.
- Building, managing and motivating large-scale teams.
- Instilling a set of common values into a disparate group.

For some of you, building, managing and motivating teams will be second nature. A number of people, however, make it to the role of Chief Executive – or at least to the table for consideration – from a functional career path. Perhaps the most likely scenario is that of the Group Finance Director. There will be certain points in the cycle when the Group Finance Director will be a very appealing prospect as the next Chief Executive – when times are hard, when there needs to be close attention to detail and emphasis on cost cutting. Equally, where there is a need to appoint someone who does not appear too partisan, the Group Finance Director can come to the fore, since he or she occupies a unique position at the heart of the business with an overview of all its constituent parts. Some organizations excel at ensuring that their top executives are given exposure to big general management roles as well as big financial roles: Unilever, Nestlé, BP immediately spring to mind as environments where individuals of real talent who have originated in the finance function would not be allowed to climb a career ladder without being given opportunities to run major projects and businesses. In other companies the Finance Director may not be so well tutored.

The stereotype of the Finance Director is of a detail-driven, controlling figure with limited imagination and less charisma. A quick glance at the FTSE 100 will undermine the stereotype – some of our most successful business figures have come through the financial route. Niall FitzGerald at Unilever, Dr Brendan O'Neill at ICI, Lord Browne at BP all came via the financial function. Jonathan Bloomer at Prudential was in the profession for many years. In fact this evidence rather supports the view that an interest in finance is a prerequisite for anyone with ambitions to lead a major enterprise, given that finance is at the very heart, is perhaps the very heart, of business. That said, there are plenty of financial directors and controllers who may not have had the quality of training and mentors or been in such sophisticated environments as those I have listed who are, perhaps, some of the most gifted business leaders of their generation. For these individuals it is particularly important to gain exposure to the management of big and broad teams. Level and scale again. Once more it may be sensible to make a lateral move in order to gain the necessary exposure.

If you are currently in a functional role you may be concerned as to what it is you need to supply in order to fill in the gaps in your skill-set. The following table addresses the most common present and missing ingredients by function. Some missing ingredients will not matter; others you will be able to do nothing about, but you may be able to address one.

Function	Strengths	Weaknesses
Group Finance Director	Financial acumen	Large-scale management
	Overview of the total business	Strategic vision
	External credentials	
	Close working relationship with some of the Non-Executives	
	Highly focused with tremendous grasp for detail	
Operations Director	Large-scale management.	Strategic overview.
	Delivery of results	External credentials/visibility
	Commercial/Financial rigour	
	Change management	
Sales and/or Marketing Director	Overview of the total business	Large-scale management
	Strategic understanding	External credentials/visibility
	Communication skills	Financial rigour
Technology Director	Overview of the total business	External credentials/visibility
	Change management	Financial rigour
	Strategic understanding	

Realistically, some disciplines better lend themselves to a direct move into a leadership position than others, notably the Finance and Operational roles. Those in R&D or Human Resources, for example, are heavily engaged in management but must generalize if they are to be considered for a leadership role.

Some tips on building and motivating a team

A little earlier in this chapter I set out, somewhat playfully, the six Cs of success. If you have those there is a fair chance that you will have what it takes to build and motivate strong teams. Additionally it helps to:

- Assume that others have the same ambitions as you and want to make the venture a success. Harness their ambition.

- Demonstrate passion and rationalism. Acknowledge the importance of facts and hard data in support of intuitions. Anchor your ideas and enable others to question, disprove or support them.

- Encourage emotion and expression – without them ideas will be stifled and spirit sapped.

- Give in with good grace. You will be wrong sometimes. Acknowledge it, give credit where it is due.

- Stick to your guns when you are right and know you are right. Leading teams involves making and standing by the right decisions.

- Let go. You do not need to be involved in all decisions. Indeed, you should save your energies for the important ones. Delegate, give others ownership and responsibility.

- Accept that you cannot be loved and respected in equal measure and settle for the latter.

- Do as you would be done by. Deal openly, fairly and calmly with all members of your team.

In the next chapter I propose to focus on the importance of trust. In this one it is sufficient to say simply that any prospective Chief Executive needs to have an instinctive under-standing of human nature. However analytically strong they may be, a good Chief Executive must listen to his or her gut and must recognize that the intuitive and instinctive feeling is often more reliable than evidence produced through lengthy analysis. Sound judgement of others and a commitment to justice are the sine qua non of good team building and motiva-tion.

The role of the headhunter

Throughout your thirties, and very possibly much of your for-ties, you will be acquiring experience and experience-related skills. You will emerge from this process a very different person from the one you were when you embarked upon it, and should have more than fulfilled your early promise. I have spent some time focusing on what the Nominations Committee will want to see, but it is worth pausing to consider the role of the headhunter once more. You may well hope to have no per-sonal need of headhunters, especially if your ambition is to secure the number one job in the organization where you have spent your entire career. The hard truth, however, is that only one person will get the top job. You may be be content to stay as a Board Director supporting the person who has beaten you in the race. Thankfully, many unsuccessful hopefuls do just this. If you are not going to be satisfied with anything less than a Chief Executive position, then you will need the help of headhunters. It may be useful to have good relationships with the leading search firms in place already so that you do not need to go out and act the supplicant but are already seen as a contender for other attractive number one posts. If you once had these, but the calls have stopped coming consider why this is? Have people stopped recommending you? Have those who have left your company forgotten you? Or have they simply assumed that you will never be moved? Does that suggest that you are complacent, or closed minded, or loyal and focused? Consider these issues – perceptions, true or false, can be maddeningly difficult to change.

It may sound as if I am simply feathering my own nest here, but I would counsel any would-be Chief Executive to maintain good relationships with headhunters throughout their career. At their best, headhunters can provide excellent career guidance and offer you insights culled from numerous boardrooms, many more than your career mentors (in general) will have had access to. Of course, headhunters enlist the help of executives in completing their searches. We find and keep track of talent by reference to other executives already known to us who, being talented themselves are likely to know talent when they see it. This informal process of networking and referral depends enormously on the good will of those we approach for advice and, as an industry, we are grateful for it and indebted to those who give us their time. I hope and believe that we offer an invaluable service in return. In some cases, those who help us become our clients. Very often they become our candidates, people we know well and can advocate strongly to our clients for a range of executive and non executive positions. In the course of their career, some executives will be helped in making a critical decision by the search fraternity and will receive coaching from people who bring a useful distance. When the phone rings from a headhunter, then, it may be worth taking the call if only to know what opportunities are in the market or to gain some insight into how you are perceived – and to correct errors.

More than this, however, it may be important to become known properly by headhunters so that they can better calibrate you against particular opportunities and so present these to you at appropriate moments. However much you want to reach the top of your chosen company, you may find that you are not being given the right opportunities to broaden. You may simply be the victim of bad luck. Perhaps there are five or six people in your cohort who are outstanding and the company is unable to provide appropriate development of all of you. You may be forced to seek your development elsewhere. Alternatively, you may be one of the preferred two or three but uneasy about your own insularity; when you are offered a new opportunity inside your company your tame headhunter will be able to help you evaluate how it will help you achieve your goal and benchmark it for you against external opportunities. Naturally, just as I would hope that headhunters use but do not abuse the good will of corporate executives, so should this service be used on a selective basis, but it is possible to establish a give and take relationship which can serve both sides.

You may be in a company where the corporate culture is so strong that it moulds and shapes executives into a pattern which is viable in that culture, but less so outside it. You may wait to attain the top job, miss out on it and then find other organizations consider you too great a risk for their board as Chief Executive. The problems of transitioning from one culture to another should never be underestimated. Sometimes it can take an executive a couple of moves to really find success. If, looking at the generation around you, you gauge that you will probably not be a front-runner in the succession plan, it may be sensible to take the plunge into unknown corporate waters while there is still time to adapt. I am certainly not saying that you cannot go from one very cohesive culture to another company as Chief Executive. Some do very successfully – but it is hard, and harder still to convince others that you can. As you move through your thirties and forties, then, you should be mindful of these factors and keep an open mind about opportunities outside the organization.

What not to do on the way up

Before moving on to a final summary of what you should have done by the end of this period of consolidation, I want to focus for a moment on what you should not have done. You should not have exploited people on the way up, stabbed people in the back or manoeuvred your way into important positions by stealth. I headed this chapter with a reference to Monopoly. When you win that game you do so by bankrupting your fellow players. Real life is a little different. You will need those you play against today as part of your team tomorrow. There is little to be gained by looking after your own interests at the expense of theirs. If you do you will pay the price in the end. Of course you will play politics – but there is a difference between careful reading and playing of the corporate politics to advance yourself and the same to ensure the fall of others. You can be a politician without being a traitor. You should not claim others' success as your own but give your team members the credit that is owed them. Equally, you should not seek to hide, disguise or pass on your failures. Instead you should remedy them and learn from them. There should be no blemish or stain attaching to you, no question about dubious morals or economy with the truth. This does not mean that you should be a saint, but you should be confident that you can reach the top by dint of your results rather than ruthlessness. Be nice to people on your way up because you may meet them on your way down!

Net achievements

What, finally, should you have done at the end of this period? What might a headhunter, as proxy for the Nomination Committee, reasonably be looking for in you? How will the experiences outlined in this chapter manifest themselves on your CV? A robust CV is one that shows breadth and depth. Headhunters look for tenure. It takes a minimum of two years to be successful in a role and to have demonstrable achievements. Naturally, you will have a certain amount of impact in your first few months in a new job and should register some quick results but time is the best test of your strategy and you should aim to demonstrate lasting results. These should be measurable. The headhunters will want to evaluate your achievements in numerical terms. By how many percentage points have you increased market share or profit margins? What were the dimensions of the business when you took it on, versus when you handed it on? Before headhunters and nominations committees come down to looking at the softer skills they will consider the hard facts of what you have done. At the end of this period you should have collected the evidence for your ability to run a major enterprise. In all probability you will have already run a substantial division. You have taken a business through change, improved it, streamlined it, revived it or built it. You will have reported to some of the most talented people in your company (or companies) and have developed some outstanding executives yourself. You will have seen different points in the business cycle and worked in large teams and small. Ideally you will have demonstrated some functional strengths as well as broad gauge general management and your local market knowledge will be off-set by broad international experience. You will be able to point to particular milestone achievements – and will be acknowledged by others for having led these initiatives. If you are destined to run a listed company of some scale you should have made it to the board by now and should, therefore, be visible. You will be known in your industry, by the relevant trade press, possibly by the analyst community and certainly by your competitors. The Non-Executives on your board will have made it their business to know you as one of the talents of your generation. In short, you will have successfully turned promise into performance. Now all that remains is to clinch the top job.

CHAPTER 5

The end game

The personal characteristics needed by the Chief Executive. How to make the transition from management to leadership. The optimal path to success focusing on mutual recognition, trust and respect between the leader and the led. The six Cs of success #2.

S o far in your career you have climbed the ladders and avoided all but the smallest snakes. You have acquired skills and experience across a range of areas to cover a host of eventualities. By now it is clear that you are a corporate master, someone with very serious ambition and, to have reached this stage, very genuine talents. This is no frivolous boardgame but a serious competition in which master pitches against master. It is a game that relies upon individual skill, knowledge, bravura ability and stamina. Your career path resembles the stages of a chess match. In the opening plays you made all the decisive choices which have enabled you to launch your middle game from a position of strength and tactical advantage. The middle game is the most complex in chess and the hardest to model because of the almost infinite permutations. The same is true of a career. Indeed, in the previous chapter which focused on that all important middle stage it was impossible to overproscribe. When to break from functional to general management, move from local to international exposure, turn from a large to a small company, these are decisions which are locally specific and no handbook can answer. Assessment of ability, decisions on quality of life – all sorts of external factors, including the calibre of the competition, will influence the middle game and determine whether you will want to remain in the contest. The end game, where there are many fewer places, becomes highly technical and can depend upon knowledge of precedent much as can the route through to the coveted top slot on the company board. Your understanding of key parts of the business can count for much in the final analysis, especially where, as the key internal candidate, you find yourself playing against someone from outside. The game of chess can suddenly radically alter, however, even at this late stage. If, for example, a pawn makes it across the board the player in charge of that pawn can reclaim a major piece and the game might be theirs. In the corporate world there is a parallel with an individual in the succession plan whose fortunes appear to be eclipsed by others. He or she can be entirely rehabilitated by the arrival or departure on the Board of a new mentor, the sudden success of a new strategy or a change in the market rendering that individual's skills at a premium against their closest competitors. Even in the end game, then, there is all to play for. Chess, like business, lends itself to endless study and there are numerous books which elucidate the moves of the masters and where particular games provide pivotal case studies. In this chapter I want to consider the mandatory skills without which you have little chance of securing success and then to set out a template for success, a case study, if you will, or game plan for making it from the bottom to the top of the organization.

As you stand on the brink of ultimate success or ultimate disappointment there is probably little left for you to do, other perhaps than to review the narrative of your career. However hard you have tried to exercise control over your career, there will be anomalies and discrepancies simply because of the devastation of contingency. You need to understand the inconsistencies, rationalize the choices you have made, both good and bad, and ensure that you can give a good account of yourself. Throughout your career you should have had periods in which you take stock, this stage – as you prepare yourself for the closest scrutiny since you joined the organization – requires open-eyed appraisal. You should know yourself well by now – this is your chance to put that knowledge to good effect. You need to be the master of your own brief, not over-rehearsed but clear and convinced.

And what should you find when you look closely at yourself? In particular, what attributes should you have acquired or honed in your career path to date? What will the nomination committee be looking to see in you when you appear before them, or indeed, the headhunters who are assessing the full field of candidates. How do you rate yourself against these broadly generic skills?

Intelligence

The quality of the mind matters most, but if you have had the benefit of first-class training in a truly rigorous subject, then you will have intellectual skills and problem-solving tools which will leverage your raw brain power. In short, if you have taken a degree in what I would term a difficult subject, then you will have acquired a pattern for learning and an analytical rubric which will stand you in excellent stead. You cannot, of course, rest on the achievements of twenty or twenty-five years ago, and you should be able to show that you have used your intelligence constructively in your working life and, importantly, that you have learned. I think it was Jack Welch who said that he began to learn how to be a Chief Executive on the day he became one, a typically illuminating remark. A mental preparedness to learn and the humility to recognize that there is much you do not know is the mark of an intelligent candidate. Under the category of intelligence there are several subcategories where you need to show strength:

- *Speed of understanding.* Time is scarce for any Chief Executive and the ability to understand things rapidly and to work out an appropriate response or to incorporate the new understanding into day-to-day action within a limited time frame is certainly useful.

- *Cutting to the essence.* An ability to grasp complex concepts and render them simple is the best test of overall intelligence I know. Your entire demeanour should indicate this trait and you will favour few well chosen words over endless bombast.

- *An ability to synthesize.* You will constantly have recourse to the expertise of others and will draw upon a wide range of sources. You will find it invaluable to be able to cut and paste the best insights to arrive at a better truth.

- *Drawing inferences.* Yours will hopefully be a subtle mind. You should be able to read between the lines, hear the nuance in the unspoken words and discern a deeper meaning. Indeed, you may be required to deliver information on occasion by the same means.

- *Intuition.* Often regarded as the antithesis of rationality, intuition, to my mind, is an intelligent response to the world around us. I have used the term judgement throughout this text and judgement is probably the rational step that follows on from the intuitive sense.

Much has been written in the last few years about emotional intelligence, of which intuition forms a part. Psychologists have written extensively on different types of intelligence. Howard Gardner, a Harvard professor and writer on leadership, has described inter- and intrapersonal intelligences thus:

> Interpersonal intelligence is the ability to understand other people: what motivates them, how they work, how to work co-operatively with them. . . . Intrapersonal intelligence is a correlative ability, turned inward. It is a capacity to form an accurate, veridical model of oneself and to be able to use that model to operate effectively in life.

The qualities of self-awareness, empathy, an understanding of the fundamental drivers motivating your action (or inaction) and those of others are all ones I would add to the list of desirable characteristics in a Chief Executive.

Personal authority and stature

This is not about physical attributes so much as the quality of self-confidence. The easiest way of describing personal authority is as a kind of self-possession. Those who have it are entirely at ease in their own skin. They know what they know and they know who they are and are comfortable with both. They have no issue in deferring to others with a superior argument and are gracious in dealing with those who do not. A Chief Executive has some of the skills of a great theatrical actor, notably timing and a strong sense of control. Take a business or political leader and put them in front of a die-hard interviewer on a prime television or radio channel and their level of personal authority will become immediately apparent. They will make their points with clarity and precision. They will listen to the alternative view (and the interviewer will in general be playing devil's advocate), but they will not allow themselves to be riled, deflected or deflated. They will surmise correctly how much they can achieve and will take as much control as is prudent. Oddly, although the net effect is of personal stature, such people are less concerned with their own performance than with ensuring that their message is appropriately delivered. The self is being controlled in the interests of the cause.

Some of this confidence comes with the job. As success piles upon success the Chief Executive relaxes into the role and enters the public domain with his standing already high. Sometimes a dose of failure helps too – the previously arrogant figure who rises phoenix-like from the ashes of corporate failure can bring some magnanimity and humility which will guarantee them a second chance. Some of this is also the product of early influences (for more on this subject see my previous book *Drive: Leadership in Business and Beyond*). The extent to which you have been loved and respected in your youth will determine the level of self-belief you have. Your early childhood experiences will instil in you a propensity or not for personal authority and stature. It may not be obvious to others that you have this quality until you are reasonably mature. If, then, you are in your early thirties and see little chance of acquiring the easy way of some of your peers and bosses, do not despair. It is not necessarily charm that you are after. Charm helps – but is not the essence of authority. You may be an intense introvert with a very focused style but minimal charm. This will not preclude you from appearing authoritative with few, well-chosen words. Indeed the Penelope Pitstops and Peter Perfects of this world with their abundant charm rarely make it through to the end of the race – for them self-regard takes the place of self-respect.

Sometimes personal authority and stature simply come from life events and from the requirement to take responsibility for others. Indeed, in your thirties and forties you are likely to have married and had children. You may have had to deal with ageing parents with poor health and you will start to see the roles between yourself and them slowly tilt into reverse. You may acquire stature from these events, from seeing yourself give support to others, from selfless love. For some personal authority and stature is a product of feeling secure with one's environment, happy perhaps. I have made the point elsewhere that happiness and complacency are the enemies of corporate success and I firmly believe that many do simply decide that there is more to life than the fight to make it to the top. For those who do not take this decision, but remain as driven as ever, the life-enhancing personal moments can provide a richness and fullness to the personality that was missing in the aggressive early years of life. Life can supply a backdrop for work which gives depth and colour to it. This is not a injunction for all would-be Chief Executives to go forth marry and multiply! Rather it is a suggestion that you keep in mind the need to have breadth in life as well as in work. If you can form strong and enduring relationships in your personal life and find an easy way of communicating across the generations, then this will feed into the relationships you can form in your business life and the ease with which you relate across the hierarchy.

Influence

Not unrelated to personal authority and stature is the matter of influence. As we noted in the first chapter, much of the appeal of a business career is that, at the very top of businesses, you can wield genuine power. A crude love of power, however, is unlikely to grant you secure tenure at the top. As the Chief Executive you will not operate in isolation but will be part of a network of interests which, to some extent, are mutually supporting and require delicate diplomacy to maintain. You will be accountable to shareholders and stakeholders and must keep in mind the interests of those parties even where they conflict. Your business may be subject to political and or fiscal decisions and you may find yourself needing to maintain close connections with international, regional, domestic or local authorities. Perhaps yours is a highly regulated industry where an understanding of those who inform regulatory policy will be imperative? In the last chapter we considered the desirability of experience and understanding of the financial community. Here we should not neglect the need for the Chief Executive to be able to influence opinion, and key points of influence will be the analysts and those running major pension funds.

In the selection process for the Chief Executive you will be given scope to exercise influence. In the first instance you will meet the impartial search firm. Next you will meet the Non-Executive Directors who comprise the Nominations

Committee first on a formal basis and, in due course, on an informal basis. I am not suggesting that carrying influence with this community will involve some cautious behind-the-scenes politicking, or ensuring that your close friends or mentors will give you good testimonials (although I know such lobbying is scarcely unusual). Rather I am simply suggesting that in your manner of conducting yourself you should demonstrate an ability to influence opinion. You should aim to make the Non-Executive Directors feel they leave their meeting with you having learnt something new. Your style should be considered, reflective, measured. You should show an understanding of the complex set of relations which support the enterprise and your cognisance of the requirement to press the claims of your own business without diminishing those of bodies allied to it.

These diplomatic skills may seem straightforward to those who have perhaps worked at the centre and been obliged to juggle conflicting interests. Most finance directors would probably not struggle particularly with this aspect of the role. For executives whose background has been highly operational and where action has been more important than negotiation the requirement to slow the pace and to give way on some apparently important points in order to secure a still greater point will seem wearisome and anathema.

Vision

Rather like emotional intelligence, vision is a slightly overused phrase in business. Without it, however, businesses are bereft. I would define vision as the stage before strategy and thus applying to the far future – perhaps five years hence. All businesses need some vision, but successful businesses, arguably, need vision more than any others. Sustaining success is very often about maintaining innovation and yet it is hard to be innovative when the business is highly successful – the 'why fix it if it ain't broke?' mentality can become synonymous with complacency. If generating a vision in a period of prosperity is hard, then it is harder still to align others with that vision. Hence vision needs to be coupled with strength of purpose and the stature and authority to render it credible.

Vision entails having a thorough understanding of the context in which the business sits. More than this, however, it requires an imaginative ability to envisage a range of different scenarios. The visionary is obsessed with the question what if? It takes courage to have vision and to bring together elements essentially unlike in possibly unholy matrimony – think of the development of Vivendi? Visionary leaders make inventive connections and spot and explore imaginative possibilities. They will pursue a hunch, but subject it to extraordinarily rigorous analysis, to find the flaw in the argument or plan. They may not be particularly consistent as they struggle with an idea, seeing its good points and bad, but once the decision is made their commitment to the idea will be absolute. During the period of indecision they will be comfortable with the uncertainty, knowing that uncertainty can give rise to novelty. This tolerance for ambiguity and even certain relish for it can make them disconcerting companions. The truth today may not be the same as the truth yesterday or the truth tomorrow. This description, in itself, seems a little at odds with the requirement for someone who is in control at the helm of the business. It should not be. The Chief Executive must be a chameleon and will don different guises for different situations.

The Nominations Committee may not be looking for someone with an extravagant vision which will change the business out of all recognition. Indeed, most would be alarmed if they were presented with such a person! They will require evidence, however, that you have been able to see beyond the immediate future in your career and have been capable of in some way extending the boundaries of the businesses you have led. If you are an external candidate you have the huge advantage of distance in relation to the business for which you are being considered as Chief Executive. Your very ignorance of the minutiae of the business represents a trap in itself and you will always be something of a risk. Alternatively, if you are the internal candidate you will be called upon to have a vision for the business which is based on intimate knowledge and too much knowledge can be just as much of a handicap as too little. Furthermore, there may be some sensitivities to be mindful of here; some members of the Nominating Committee may well feel implicated by any implied criticism you may make of the present strategy.

From management to leadership

If you have acquired a good portion of the experience set out in Chapter 4 and overlaid that with some of the skills alluded to above, then there is a some chance that you have what it takes to make the transition from excellent manager to true leader. I have already noted that the Chief Executive does not operate in splendid isolation, but is at the centre of a complex web of relationships. I have also alluded to the much-vaunted concept of 'emotional intelligence'. There is little question that you cannot judge a Chief Executive (or an aspiring Chief Executive) in isolation but must consider them in the context of the people around them and the broader setting of the environment they occupy. So far we have considered experience and skills. The missing piece in the jigsaw is perhaps attitude.

Nick Binnedel, head of the Gibbs Garden Institute of Business Science in South Africa, gave me an idea for a grid demonstrating the essential components of how leaders gain our respect and trust, and in turn win our co-operation, flexibility, adaptability and loyalty. I have modified this slightly, but believe it is a useful way of considering the various stages, which are broadly speaking, consecutive and cumulative.

Education and learning
↓
Experience and knowledge
↓
Performance and delivery
↓
Recognition
↓
Respect
↓
Trust
↓
Co-operation, flexibility, adaptability and loyalty

In the first three phases we see the experiential – the steps we take and the skills we acquire. The remainder are attitudinal.

He or she who passes through these various stages will emerge a fully rounded figure who is not only equipped to take on the role but perceived to be so by those around them. Indeed, they have acquired external validation. They will be, in short, a whole person, rounded emotionally as well as experientially reliable.

The appointment of a Chief Executive is a contract between parties – between the individual on the one hand and the organization on the other. A would-be Chief Executive who loses sight of the need for reciprocity will also lose sight of the chance to lead. The above chart shows the effect of the individual upon an organization. If that individual can successfully win the recognition, respect and trust of the organization and, equally, can demonstrate the same towards the organization and those in it, then the output will be a flexible workforce. In short, you get out what you put in.

The early, experiential stages

In Chapter 1 it emerged that education can be of varying degrees of usefulness for those who pursue a dream to run a major enterprise and we observed that entrepreneurs tend to eschew formal education in their haste to pursue their own ideas. Equally, history is awash with self-made men, autodidacts, who lacked formal education but made up for it with a tremendous passion for learning and knowledge. Education provides many of us with the tools for learning; we learn how to express ourselves in an orderly and evocative fashion. We learn how to construct an argument, to understand the relationship between cause and effect and how to uncover hidden facts through research. Composition, comparison, connection –

education gives us all this, and much besides. Most important, however, is a thrill for learning and a veritable thirst for knowledge. Education can inspire this but sometimes, can stifle it too. Some who miss out on formal education develop a relish for learning that they pass on to others. We are all familiar with people whose parents, having missed out on formal education, have instilled in their children both a drive to be educated but, more importantly, perhaps, an unquenchable thirst to acquire knowledge. The common factor among successful people, it seems to me, is this insatiable curiosity thats roam over everything both practical and intellectual characterized by constant questioning. How does this work? Why does this happen? What if I do this? The mark of a good candidate can often be the quality of the questions they ask. Indeed, sometimes we can learn more from the questions of others than we do from the information they provide, and a good manager, much like a good teacher, will tease out better work from those in his or her team by asking the right questions at the right moment.

No amount of education and learning will make you into a Chief Executive without considerable experience. This second phase concerns the application of education and learning in order to acquire true expertise or competence in one or more chosen areas. We never stop acquiring experience and learning but in the early days of a career our focus is entirely upon gaining mastery. Later on our interests must inevitably become more diffuse. On moving from a graduate training scheme, the young executive will identify an area which both interests them and where they have some applicable skills. Over the coming years they will establish themselves as truly expert, achieving innovations, demonstrating aptitude ahead of others, penetrating into the mysteries of the subject deeper than others, achieving results which are more robust than their peers. Sometimes, the far-seeing executive will recognize that a particular function will have primacy in the future and will enter that area often to the mystification of their peers who will choose the functions which are recognized as primary at that time. Twenty or thirty years ago it must have seemed an unlikely choice to move into technology, to identify with the geeks rather than the governing class in the corporation. Ten or fifteen years ago the logistics and supply chain will have seemed similarly unlikely destinations for top talent. Nevertheless, excellent Chief Executives have come through from both sources. In part this is because it is always easier to make your mark, if you are talented, where you face little competition. More than this, however, the very novelty of both disciplines will have held particular appeal for those with most developed learning skills and the absence of precedent will have, in turn, enabled innovation. Rules can restrict and established disciplines rapidly acquire entire rule books. The most talented, visionary future Chief Executives are often those who become the rule makers in new areas or the rule breakers in traditional functions in need of revivifying. The dot-com bubble has now burst and we have all become accustomed to thinking that the internet is no more than another distribution channel. It is likely, however, that we will find in ten years time that the whole arena will yield some of our more accomplished Chief Executives who cut their teeth in an area which allowed them to experiment, and experience failure as well as success. The experience phase of the career should be about experimentation. It may take some time to find something that really sparks an interest. Indeed, some people may only acquire the dream to be a Chief Executive when they find in themselves a great passion for a particular area. There comes a point at which experimentation spills into dilettantism but some trial and error is healthy. A number of very successful Chief Executives may achieve their first successes relatively late and here the fact that they are coming from behind may supply some of the drive that will fuel their later crowning success.

Having acquired experience, the Chief Executive must next convert that expertise into real achievements. Performance and delivery follow logically from the mastery that comes with experience. For a future Chief Executive this phase is about impact and effect. Performance must be exemplary and delivery go far beyond expectation. This is the point at which the most talented in an organization suddenly reveal themselves. They mastermind a particular project, initiate a new deal or develop a groundbreaking campaign. Whatever the nature of the achievement, it will have significant impact on the company. You will be identified with it and it will be a milestone in your career.

Recognition

Achievements count for little if they are not recognized as such. Recognition is an important phase in the progress of a nascent Chief Executive. The word conveys a sense of discovery and realization and this phase marks a move away from the experiential towards the attitudinal as both the corporation and the individual recognize the importance of the executive to the company. That importance derives not just from exemplary performance and outstanding competence and achievements but from a recognition, on both sides, of shared values, or values that are consistent with the aspirations of the organization. This is the moment when the executive will feel a sense of arrival, of being in the right place with the right people at the right time. He or she will feel a sense of their own ability to influence the course of the organization, to have a positive, lasting impact.

In the first instance, however, it is your achievements which will earn you recognition. People around you will acknowledge that your's was the first inspiration, or that the implementation owed everything to your skill. Your name will attach to the achievement and you will move from having potential to having proven it, at least in one area. A recognition of shared values will come from the manner in which you conduct yourself, from your relationships with others and the style in which you have executed your particular success. You will have been clear, open, encouraging but critical where necessary. You will have set clear boundaries, but enabled people to stretch them. You will have reinforced the positive values of the organization and will emerge from the process as someone people understand to be exemplary and representative of the culture.

Sometimes recognition is not instantaneous. Individuals may do a number of small things simply because they are not so situated to accomplish high-profile achievements. Possibly your function is dominated more by process and service than by events in which case you may wait longer for your moment. Word of mouth, however, is generally a very efficient method of communication. Word will simply get around that you are talented. People will wait and watch and, bearing in mind the desire on the part of the organization to enable its talented staff, you will be given your opportunity. Occasionally recognition may be retrospective. Where an organization fails to recognize talent and give due credit then the executive concerned may be obliged to leave and find recognition elsewhere. The impact of what they have done may become apparent belatedly, but too late for the organization to take full advantage of the talent that was in their midst. And very often recognition will be surprising. Not infrequently, this is the moment when the maverick or the outsider comes to the fore. Perhaps you are a little different from the rest of the cohort who joined the organization when you did, or from those on the same reporting line? That difference or distance may lend you a clearer perspective than those who are very close to the prevailing norms. You may be able to penetrate mysteries that are opaque to others and to articulate what you see in ways that startle but also spark others.

This process of recognition is a vital stage in the development of a senior executive. Some perfectly capable executives simply never find their milieu or moment and so are not empowered and trusted by the organization sufficiently to affect its future. In essence recognition is a platform from which to perform. It marks the organization's acceptance of you as fitted to lead.

Respect

Implicit in the term recognition is respect. In the act of recognizing an achievement we are, in general, conferring respect upon an individual. It is not enough for a would-be Chief Executive to accept the respect of others; he or she must feel respect in turn. We do not do our best work where we do not have respect for the overall objectives of the endeavour. Where that respect is missing it is better to walk away and seek it elsewhere before a lack of respect equates to a lack of conviction, vacillation and a failure to lead. The process of respect, then, must be recipro-cal. Those who incur our respect are those who, likewise, show us some. We respect our leaders because we see in them some-thing that we neither see in others nor do we see in ourselves. Our willingness to follow them, however, may be dissipated if we do not feel from them some degree of reciprocity. They must respect what we bring to the equation. Our labour, our skills, our commitment. Without us the leader is nothing. There can be no leader without followers, after all. In corporate terms there is little that anyone can achieve in isolation and a sign of brilliance is an ability to enrol others into a particular project, to energize, galvanize and inspire.

Very often entrepreneurs excel in this area. Richard Branson walks into a building and makes those around him feel very special. He respects their competence, their energy and their willingness to work for him. Entrepreneurs, because they are not necessarily from conventional backgrounds and may not have trodden the conservative route through school, univer-sity and blue-chip companies, may be less likely to demand orthodoxy in others. Also, when entrepreneurs start a com-pany they do not have the luxury of choice. Company founders will staff their business with those who are willing to join them, irrespective of the risk or initially more limited ben-efits than they might achieve in an established concern. The entrepreneur buys loyalty, sometimes over expertise, and very often he pays back with loyalty. Many an entrepreneur sur-rounds himself, even when the business has multiplied many times over, with those who started out with him. Implicit in this loyalty is a recognition that success is not achieved in solitude but as part of a multifaceted team.

Corporations tend to disperse teams far more rapidly than occurs in new entrepreneurial ventures. This is inevitably so as able and ambitious young executives demand development, movement and momentum in their career. By accommodating the ambitions of their staff companies ensure that they can draw upon a constant supply of new staff who are drawn to the organization because of its reputation for offering opportunity. It is rare, then, that we see relationships in organizations enduring over many years and such stability may not even be desirable. Sometimes we see a boss and secretary moving together through a corporation and from one corporation to another. They have built up a mutual dependence. In so far as it ever wise for a person in authority to give way to this level of interdependence such a relationship is almost paradigmatic of good working relations between a manager/leader and his/her team. The each supplies to the other something that they cannot themselves provide.

Respect is hard won and easily lost. Success can go to the head of some who fail to recognize that they owe others recognition for their part in that success. The executive who starts to feel he is omniscient will rapidly lose the respect of others in the firm and may end up a laughing-stock. Having won the respect of others, executives must work to retain it, always according the respect that is due. An executive who issues a reprimand to a member of staff who is somehow reneging on their responsibilities will not be thanked for so doing, certainly will not be liked but, provided there is justice in their case, they will be respected for it. Indeed, justice is at the heart of respect. The executive who gives his staff niggardly bonuses but awards himself handsomely will lose respect on the dual grounds that he has been self-serving and unfair. Fine for the boss to take more – it is understood that he should – but not at the expense of those who may not have put him at the top but certainly contribute to him staying there.

Respect should not be confused with liking. Great visionaries are seldom liked – their vision very often disconcerts and in thinking differently they suggest that all is not right with the status quo which undermines those who see no fault with that status quo. One of the greatest visionaries of the twentieth century must surely have been Alan Turing. It is not over-stating things to say that his role in breaking the German Enigma code was pivotal in the Allied success in World War Two. His vision underpins the entire development of the computer. In an act of homage, the founders of Apple Computer chose the company's name as a reference to the apple Turing impregnated with poison, and their logo depicts the same apple with his fatal bite taken from it. This great mark of respect acknowledges a man whose greatness, little recognized at the time, is fully recognized now. He was neither particularly well liked, nor particularly well understood, but Turing engendered respect in others. He thought things others could not think and did things others would not do. He thought and acted better than most others in his chosen field. For this he incurred lasting respect. Few corporations are likely to give us visionaries of Turing's stature, but the point remains a valid one. Respect should operate independently of sentiment.

Trust

Where respect is established trust should follow. Perhaps there is no more important concept in business than this. The inter-related nature of commerce means that one enterprise relies upon another for vital materials and services and very often cannot exist other than in relation to a major supplier. The two businesses are interdependent but very different, with different priorities and objectives at different times. It is trust that enables them to co-exist and to co-operate. On a local level, in any given organization the various departments are inter-dependent. A sales office cannot make a commitment to a customer which cannot then be met by manufacturing. Some-times the goodwill and understanding between sales and production can break down, the commitments made by sales are not met and the customer moves elsewhere with the loss of revenues to the business and just as important, the loss of good-will and reputation. By and large such internecine conflict is avoided because of a fair measure of trust from one side to the other. When we give another person a task to do on our behalf we cannot know that they will do it to our satisfaction, but we must trust that they will.

In his excellent book entitled *Trust*, Francis Fukuyama demon-strates that the practice of trusting may be socially and historically conditioned. He talks of associative cultures where a common concern will bring together groups that otherwise have different motives and priorities. Out of that common concern comes trust. From that trust comes an econ-omy where it is possible to build large-scale enterprises and networks of large-scale enterprises. His point that trust is hard to develop is extremely well-made, as is that bigger point that, without it, we cannot work together and build lasting organizations. We all experience trust in our personal lives. When we are betrayed by one person we find it hard to trust them again but we also find it hard to trust others who may act similarly towards us. In order to trust people we must risk ourselves, risk hurt and disappointment. As with so much else, it is advisable to develop the habit of trusting others early. In infancy we have little choice; we are obliged to trust those who care for us for our very survival. Through play with siblings and friends we develop the instinct to trust further but if we are repeatedly let down then we may elect to rely upon ourselves and not to turn to others. This can have devastating effects in our later life. If we trust nothing and no one we may see fault in any collective and become spoilers. We may be motivated by a requirement to support the self and engage in collective activities simply to that end, becoming ultimately self-serving and ungenerous. We neither trust those above us in an enterprise or those below us and cannot function.

Building trust is not a matter for a moment. It comes with time and with track record. Trust follows on from respect but does not do so automatically. Trust cannot be manufactured but must be earned. Trust is fundamental, particularly in a world such as business where there is little or no democracy. Those who make the mistake of thinking that they can manipulate others to earn their trust usually discover their folly eventually. The person who shifts allegiance according to the prevailing winds of favour or the boss who is critical of some staff to others will generally be found out. In organizations people talk and share confidences and the fickle friend or the false boss will rapidly be revealed. Organizations which encourage mentoring are likely to be ones where trust will flourish. A sense of concern for others, a willingness to help and create opportunities, coupled with a preparedness to offer constructive advice, not shying away from hard truths; these skills in a mentor reflect a culture which is straightforward and open. Candour is perhaps the biggest tool you can employ in building trust. At annual appraisal time be open and honest with others regarding their prospects. If you cannot meet the career aspirations of some, of if the aspirations of others are misplaced telling them so will earn their short-term disappointment but their longer term respect and trust.

Building trust in an organization is dependent on some understanding of how organizations function. An organization serves a wide community but it serves no one individual. The good manager or leader in whom people place their trust is one who sees that he or she owes his allegiance to the organization first and the individual second. Where the interests of organization and individual coincide, then all is well and good. Where they are at variance then the organization comes first. You may like the person who is working hard but, ultimately, not delivering the results but you cannot keep them *in situ* simply out of sentiment. You owe it to the individual concerned to manage the process with sensitivity and tact (and also with candour) but you owe it to the organization to resolve the problem. Indeed, you owe it to the team since a small group will no more tolerate a weak link than a large. This will seem harsh. When Jack Welch published his memoirs the media made much of his early days as 'Neutron Jack'. Certainly he made large numbers of people redundant. In doing so he created opportunities for many more and, along the way, created one of the world's super success stories (in business terms at any rate). We do not criticize a gardener who carefully prunes and trims a plant in order that the new shoots may flourish. We encourage and applaud such prudent husbandry. The same is true in business. Pruning a plant is a little different from cutting a swathe through an organization. The gardener hardly need concern himself with serious casualties; the corporate manager must be equipped to deal with the pain of those who the company can no longer accommodate. Nevertheless, if sentiment gets in the way and individual needs become more important than corporate, then, ultimately, the corporation will suffer.

Building trust can become highly complex in an entrepreneurial venture, where the fortunes and identity of the entrepreneur are so intimately bound up with one another as to be, at times, virtually indistinguishable. I have already alluded to the entrepreneur who loyally stands by his staff even as the company grows. Where the founder stands by his staff as the company outgrows their strengths he will be taking a risk with the organization which could well lead to its demise. Better by far to be open about the natural course of a growing business and the need to bring in managers with different skills and to set in place very substantial rewards so that people can leave the business properly compensated and with their self-respect intact. Trust, after all, is founded on respect and not on pity and where people suspect they are being retained because of pity they will lose trust and feel patronized. Trust indeed, calls for real empathy with others, an ability to put yourself in someone else's position and act accordingly.

Trust requires a delicate balance between maintaining accountability and giving others autonomy and ownership. Delegation is not about abrogation of responsibility. We free people to perform well where they know that we will stand by them both in their successes and failures. The manager will take credit for the successes of his or her team, successes which may owe something to the freedom they have been given to innovate and experiment. So should he or she also take responsibility on the occasions when that freedom leads to failure. The extent to which individuals want autonomy and freedom will vary dramatically within a team. All the more reason for the exercise of empathy, for an imaginative understanding of what motivates those around you.

Most of us exercise trust on a fairly local level. We trust and are trusted by our partners, friends, immediate bosses and subordinates. A Chief Executive must establish trust on a public level, with shareholders and stakeholders. The community with which the Chief Executive must engage is a highly varied one, separated by geography, generation and frequently interests. In addition to the shareholders it includes the Board, the employees, customers, unions and very often national or local authorities. The challenge will be to maintain principles, to be seen by all people as having manifest integrity even when the decisions and views the Chief Executive expresses may run counter to a particular group's direct interests. No Chief Executive can ever be all things to all people, nor should he strive to be, but while he can try to accommodate some interests, those of the organization must take priority. This might suggest that the interests of the shareholders hold sway given that the primary duty of an organization is to make profits for the benefit of investors. There will be occasions, however, where short-term shareholder gain will be postponed in the interests of the longer term security of the business. Ultimately, assuming the strategy is correct this will lead to greater returns for shareholders or greater shareholder security. The Chief Executive will be given the space to pursue his particular strategy in direct proportion to the amount of trust he engenders amongst these different groups. A little earlier I considered the emotional strengths and attributes needed and, differently glossed, these same six Cs of success apply here.

The six Cs of success #2

- *Courage* – the courage to stand alone and to operate rationally and without giving way to sentiment but also to admit when wrong or when a better truth is revealed. The courage to subjugate personal benefits to those of the organization.
- *Certitude* – vacillation is the enemy of success. The Chief Executive must be someone who can be relied upon to come to a considered, measured decision and be steadfast with it.
- *Consistency* – able to deal with all people evenly, showing neither prejudice nor preferential treatment, but taking each situation on its own merits.
- *Confidence* – having the emotional reserves to assess others, rate and judge them and operate with them without being either threatened or overawed.

- *Clarity* – candour and straightforwardness engender trust where ambiguity and deviousness generate only uncertainty and mistrust. The skill here is to know when to offer a view and when not and, in withholding one, to be open that this is what you are doing.
- *Calm* – mood swings and vicissitudes of temper ricochet through an organization. The Chief Executive should better aim to be the still point around which all others turn.

We might add a seventh C to this list, without which none of these others will have much effect and that is competence. A Chief Executive who regularly demonstrates *competence* will find trust a part of his portion, especially at times of uncertainty and risk.

Co-operation, flexibility, adaptability and loyalty

Once the executive has moved through the stages from education and learning to trust they have assembled the co-ordinates for leadership. The ultimate output of these experiences, skills and attitudes will be a healthy organization, one that is adapted for leadership – for your leadership. Once you have made it and are the annointed Chief Executive it becomes all the more important to keep with you the lessons that you have learnt on your way up. The organization is an organism of which you are the head, but a head without the limbs, the nerves, the blood and organs is redundant. Lose sight of this and you lose sight of success.

A co-operative organization is one that recognizes the rights of the individuals within it, but also recognizes that these are subservient to the overall purpose of the organization. People work together through a form of enlightened self-interest. If they perpetuate the interests of the organization they are perpetuating their own interests. This presupposes that they agree with the underlying purpose of the enterprise but a co-operative organization spots and acts upon those in its midst who do not share the overall objectives. To continue the metaphor, a healthy organization will develop a strong immune system which will fight threats to its well-being. An organization which is accustomed to co-operation is one where people continually draw up and review contracts between themselves, giving a little in one place to receive in another. This process of negotiation is open and understood and by being so leaves no place for politics and back-biting. It also gives rise to a sense of possibility resting on the foundation of certainty; we know that we can work this out collectively therefore we can take more risks. An organization has access to the combined skills and talents of many hundreds, often many thousands of people. If it can bring these together in a vital organism where the actions of one give rise to the actions of another then it will be an efficient machine, one that can learn, grow and adapt. Comparisons with the body or with a machine, however, fall down. An organization is, in some ways, a more complex organism than either. Bodies and machines have a fixed structure and neither will tolerate much mutation. Organizations have the capability for metamorphosis, for regeneration and rebirth. They depend for this, however, on the rich accumulation of trust and respect, on a preparedness throughout the organization to learn and to continue learning and for these qualities to be manifest in the persons at the top.

I began this chapter with a reference to chess. The parallel is a good one. The game is one where there are a number of clearly laid out moves which the conscientious and ambitious player can master and adopt. With careful focus and study a novice can go a considerable way towards mastery of the subject. A master, however, achieves ultimate success not by dint of having digested precedent, or even by superb strategy. In the end the master will achieve that status by dint of superior mental strengths, by force of character. He will respect his opponents, never underestimate them, but under close and constant scrutiny will keep a cool, clear head and win, in part through resolve. The endgame in a corporate career may take place over a number of months or even years as the Board quietly assesses you and your key internal competitors plus, perhaps, one or two from outside. You have none of the advantage of the master chess-player since you do not necessarily know the identity of your opponents and cannot scrutinize their every move. This in itself calls for tremendous reserves of resolve; requiring you to work not in reaction to another but on your own terms and those of the organization. In the end the challenge to secure the prize of Chief Executive may seem less like a game of chess than a game of solitaire – you and only you can control the moves.

CHAPTER 6

Game over or match replay?

The choices open to you if you have failed at the first attempt. How to assess whether or not you should try again. Positioning yourself with the successful Chief Executive, with the Board and with headhunters. On being a non executive yourself, aspiring towards Chairmanship. The benefits of a pluralist career. On being a business angel. Some differences between small, medium sized and large organizations – knowing where you might fit.

orget games of skill and strategy, games where stamina and mastery count. For some the outcome of the contest to be a Chief Executive will be bitter disappointment. Then, the entire tournament will seem more like a game of roulette, entirely dominated by that great imponderable: chance. Ask any successful person to outline the factors in their success and they will tell you that luck features prominently. Look closely at those people who nearly made it – there are politicians aplenty through history who *nearly* made it. Similarly entertainers. More often than not ill fortune was partly their downfall. Not being in the right place at the right time. Changing fashions. The same holds true in business. The Board may take a strategic decision to skip a generation in its succession planning, giving the incumbent time to round off his achievements while the heir is then ensured a reasonable tenure in which to notch up achievements in his turn. Possibly the Board has taken the view that having gone inside on the last three occasions for the Chief Executive they want an entirely different perspective this time around. There may be endless reasons why someone else was selected. Perhaps you were too closely associated with the outgoing incumbent. Or possibly the Board simply made the wrong decision. Perhaps they did not; perhaps there was someone who simply seemed better suited for the challenge of the day. Maybe you were one of a particularly talented group of directors. Judged against a different group you might have been the victor.

Counting the emotional cost

I would not underestimate the emotional cost of participating in a succession battle. It may be faintly incendiary of me to use the term battle. There is scarcely all-out warfare between competing candidates and, it is to be hoped, few skirmishes. Nevertheless, this is a conflict where the outcome counts. By this stage it seems more than a mere game, even of the most competitive variety. These are quite often protracted affairs, especially where the search is conducted across the world's markets. It takes time to woo outsiders who may not be familiar with the challenges the organization offers. The internal candidates may feel in a state of suspension while a separate group of challengers is assembled. They may also feel that there is inequality in a situation where outsiders are wooed and those inside the business must, effectively, do the wooing. Here all the stock of emotional strength and tolerance for ambiguity which is required of a Chief Executive will be extremely useful as you try to work in an artificial situation. It is possible that those around you will be aware of your ambitions, especially if, for whatever reason, the search is in the public domain. This is a pressure in itself; it is disconcerting to have people aware of our desires, however reasonable they may be. Equally it is uncomfortable to know that people are speculating about your chances, enjoying the spectacle and possibly even revelling in the outcome. The process is a debilitating one. It is to be hoped that the organization will manage the process with sensitivity and speed, limiting any publicity and ensuring, in so far as possible, that the process is transparent. You should, for example, be given exactly the same treatment as the external candidates, shown the necessary literature and be kept informed regarding the timetable. You should also be clear regarding the Board's approach and the rationale behind that approach. Even so, you will be called to give an account of yourself both to outsiders and to those with whom you may have been working for some years. We all know that it can be harder to reveal oneself to people we know than it is to do so to complete strangers. Assuming you have come through the business, or joined the organization mid-career then this will be the first time for some considerable period that you have been called upon to justify your actions. More importantly, since actions are easily discussed, this will probably be the first time in many years that you have been asked to lay yourself open to scrutiny of an intense nature concerning matters usually confined to the privacy of your thoughts. The process of selecting a Chief Executive can be, quite simply intrusive. It is to be hoped that it is never offensive, but assuming the company takes its responsibilities very seriously, your motivation will be closely examined and you will be called upon to set out the factors which have made you the person you are. The search firm and the Nominations Committee will be interested in the factors beyond work (which, after all, they have some insight into) and may probe far back into your early life. While some people feel comfortable with this process of self-revelation they are in the minority. Most serious candidates for Chief Executive roles have a persona which is their shell. The search process removes this shell and lays them bare.

Understanding the decision

If you are the successful candidate then all this agony will have been worthwhile. Suddenly it will seem preordained that you be the winner, inevitable from the first moment you joined the organization. You have been through the most testing assessment of your life and been judged the best. Your self-belief will have been ratified, your effort rewarded. For the moment, at least, you can feel thoroughly satisfied with yourself.

But if you are the unsuccessful candidate you will feel the reverse of this. You will feel disappointment. Perhaps you will feel embarrassment or humiliation, maybe even betrayal; this job should have been yours. Possibly you will feel resentment and envy. Some will simply shrug their shoulders and accept that it was not to be. But not all. This may feel like rejection of a very fundamental kind. You have identified very strongly with this business and it has favoured someone else. It is to be hoped that you will have been carefully de-briefed concerning the decision. At the very least you need to establish:

- Why you have been unsuccessful. Was this situational. Did the board simply decide they needed a different set of experiences? Was the chosen candidate more appropriate for the moment or more talented?
- In what ways did you appear a weaker candidate? Were there specific issues raised by the Nominations Committee?

- Was it a close-run thing? How did you measure up against the external candidates?

This is not the moment to be anything other than honest with yourself. How realistic was your bid to be the Chief Executive? Perhaps you entered the race a little early? Has the Nominations Committee made the right decision? If they have chosen an internal candidate then you will be able to make a considered judgement here. If not you need to understand something of the person who has been judged a better choice than you. Any failure is an opportunity to learn and to think carefully about your next move.

Part of your decision will depend on your age. You are likely to be in your forties or fifties. It is possible you are in your thirties, but unlikely. Indeed, if you have been a part of a succession race in a listed company while still in your thirties (subject to the size of the business, of course) you can consider yourself to have done exceptionally well to have merited consideration. It is likely, also, that you did indeed enter the race too early. While there are no hard and fast rules about the age at which people should run listed companies, and while there is no direct correlation between age and talent, it is reasonable to suggest that maturity, which can indeed be age and experience related, is a skill worth having. It is certainly the case that many of the world's largest companies look for some twenty years' experience, and very often thirty, before elevating people to the level at which they can be considered for succession as Chief Executive. If you are in your mid-forties you will have a couple of choices:

1.   You can start to look outside. If you have come second on a shortlist for a significant listed business you will not lack opportunities to be a number one.

2.   You can remain in the company.

Option 2: staying in the company

If you select the second of the two options it is a fair supposition that you will not become the number one. In all probability the newly appointed Chief Executive will be much the same age as you and so, when next the succession is under debate, it will be the generation immediately below you who will provide the contenders. Of course, there is always the possibility that the Chief Executive will leave. David Simon, now Lord Simon, when number two at BP, famously took up the baton after the surprise departure of Sir Robert Horton. Perhaps the new incumbent will fail. If the appointment has been made from outside the business the chances of failure are heightened and, where that happens, a Board having burnt its fingers once is far more likely to look inside for succession. Of course, as someone with significant emotional investment (and very likely financial investment too) in the business you would not want the successful candidate to fall at the first hurdle. If, however, you are absolutely convinced that the wrong choice was made you may want to wait and see what will happen. Should this be a fair representation of how you feel, I would venture to suggest that *you* will fail before the new incumbent. A high level of disaffection will make it impossible for you to maintain the standard of work necessary to remain one of the chosen few most likely to be involved in the selection process on another occasion. Your best advice would be to put the disappointment behind you and accelerate your search for a new career.

I shall assume, however, that once the first disappointment has worn off, you will take a far more measured and sanguine approach. You may, upon mature reflection, believe that the process has been an illuminating one. You may have learnt something about yourself, or come to accept something that you knew in your heart but had not confirmed in your mind. The decision may well have been correct. Quite possibly you are a natural number two and not a natural number one at all. There is no shame in this. In some ways the number two in a major enterprise is very likely to be a more rounded person than the number one. I have written repeatedly in these pages that part of the quest to be a Chief Executive should involve a quest to be as rounded a person as possible. I might appear to be contradicting myself, therefore, by suggesting that the number two, who in this context we are positioning as the failed number one, is the more rounded. In truth, my over-whelming belief, based on meetings with numerous Chief Executives is that while you cannot depend upon much in the make-up of a Chief Executive, you can certainly depend on a degree of difference. Many of the people who become Chief Executives have large, powerful strengths; they often have important weaknesses. Being rounded is not what they are selected for. Being successful over a period is what it is about. Being successful, however, depends to some extent on being as rounded as possible. The terms as possible are important ones here. As I said at the outset of this book, to be the number one you must have an extraordinary degree of drive, commit-ment and capacity for sacrifice. I do not want to set Chief Executives on pedestals and suggest that they are super-beings; they are not. All the same, they have a certain passion and fire – however well contained and quietly expressed –

which snaps at them and sets them apart from the rest of us. The number two does not have the same sense of urgency, lacks the inner demons, and so has time and mental energy left over to focus on things outside the immediate concern of business. A natural number two may well lack the vision of the natural number one, may well be too well grounded in the present and the here and now to be able to look to the far future and to venture beyond the horizon. Nevertheless that rootedness in the present can be an absolutely invaluable asset in an organization, especially where the number one is of a particularly visionary cast of mind. Indeed, a number two, by being ballast for such a number one, can be the means by which both the number one is enabled to succeed and the corporation is protected from the worst excesses of the visionary imagination.

The Chief Operating Officer

In the United States there exists a clearly defined role which is effectively the second in command. The role is that of the Chief Operating Officer (COO), or Group Managing Director to use the British phrase. Increasingly the role is being exported to Europe and is certainly becoming more common in Anglo-Saxon businesses. It might carry the title Group Managing Director. This is a pivotal role in an organization and the natural home for the number two. The Chief Operating Officer must have a strong collaborative relationship with the Chief Executive Officer but will offer complementary skills. The concerns of the Chief Operating Officer focus on the framework, processes and systems which pertain in the business and ensuring that these are optimized, reviewed and, if necessary, re-engineered. Where the Chief Executive is concerned with strategy and vision, the Chief Operating Officer must be concerned with the mechanisms which will facilitate that strategy and vision. The role involves problem solving, planning, analysis and ensuring that structures, rules and behaviours are consistent with delivery. It is the primary management, as distinct from leadership, role in the business. A Chief Operating Officer is not automatically debarred from becoming the Chief Executive Officer, quite the contrary, some are Chief Executive Officers in waiting. If we assume that the company wishes to retain you and to remotivate you, then to make you the Chief Operating Officer is an excellent way of continuing to provide momentum in your career and, importantly, an opportunity to learn more.

The focus of the Chief Operating Officer's role is an internal one, unlike the Chief Executive who looks outwards. It can provide a great training ground to be a number one. He or she must be acquainted with external factors affecting the performance of the business but is not engaged in the external representation of the business with shareholders and the financial community. Instead his or her primary focus will be on the various constituent parts of the enterprise. Indeed, the key reports into the Chief Operating Officer will include all the divisional directors, any operations, manufacturing or supply chain directors. Indeed, all those functions which are concerned with the day-to-day delivery of product are likely to fall within the remit of the Chief Operating Officer. Those which have a more strategic focus or are concerned with external perceptions will be likely to report to the Chief Executive (such as Finance, Strategy, Human Resources, Sales and Marketing, Customer Service). The Chief Operating Officer must have operational credibility in order to challenge the Chief

Executive Officer's thinking where necessary from a position of genuine practical knowledge. That operational credibility will also give credence to the strategy since he will be the major conduit by which the Chief Executive will disseminate that strategy across the business. A high level of comfort with detail, strong logical and rational skills and a persuasive personal style are critical components in the person of the Chief Operating Officer. Is he a real Chief Executive or will he only ever be a Chief Operating Officer? Maybe a young Chief Operating Officer has the potential to become a Chief Executive Officer but an older Chief Operating Officer probably never will.

One of the features which distinguishes a natural number two from a natural number one is that the former is prepared to suppress his or her ego in the service of the number one. It is not necessarily the case that the number two will shun the spotlight, rather he or she will decide that the spotlight better belongs to the number one, that there is a better business case for it. Arguably the number two is paradigmatic of corporate man. The interests of the corporation will always come before the interests of the self. With the Chief Executive the interests of the corporation do not come before those of the self; rather the two are consanguinous. Being the number two does not preclude being the number one. In the United States it is sometimes the Chief Operating Officer who will succeed the Chief Executive Officer to the number one slot as the best of the internal candidates. Some people, however, are better suited to the role as a number two. They facilitate. They make things happen. They work in partnership. A great number two is almost as precious as a good number one.

The apprentice chairman?

It may be the case that you are currently the Group Finance Director. While you may lack the operational breadth of some of your counterparts, which may make it more difficult to secure a Chief Executive position in another company, there is another role for which you are, potentially, highly suited. For you, the role of Chairman may be as valid an aspiration as the role of Chief Executive.

Consider the job specification of a chairman.

Chairman – responsibilities

*   To lead the Board.
*   To put in place the procedures to govern the Board's work.
*   To ensure the Board fully discharges its duties.
*   To schedule all meetings for the Board and, working closely with the Committee Chairmen, schedule meetings for committees.
*   Establish and set the agenda for the all meetings of the Board in consultation with the Directors providing input.
*   Ensure the proper flow of information to the Board; assessing the adequacy and timing of these materials such as to ensure that communication across the Board is maximized.
*   Act as a liaison point for members of the Board and members of the management team.
*   Ensure that adequate time is allocated to enable due consideration of key business matters.
*   Ensure that Board decisions can be appropriately imple-

mented by allocating specific tasks to specific individuals.

- Represent the company to the external groups, working closely with the Chief Executive.
- Working closely with the Committee Chairmen, ensure that the processes are in place to enable the committees to fulfil their functions to a high standard.
- Take responsibility for the recruitment and, where necessary, development and retention of Directors and the Chief Executive.
- Act as a key adviser to Board members and, in particular, as sounding-board and mentor to the Chief Executive.

One of the key aspects of the Chairman's role is that of external representation. This, of course, is the particular strength of the Finance Director. Indeed, there are few elements of this role that seem alien to that of any talented Group Finance Director. The Chairman and the Group Finance Director are both concerned with process, with communication and with enabling. Both require extraordinary commercial acumen. Both are advisers and sounding-boards to the Chief Executive. In general the Chairman is an elder statesman figure; his advice will reflect longer service in business, greater depth of service on boards and a certain detachment which comes from distance. A Finance Director may logically aspire to be a Chairman. Assuming you can acquire additional board experience there is a strong case to be made that you, currently the Finance Director may be particularly well-suited to move directly to a Chairman's role.

If then, you have assessed your situation and realistically understand that your greater skills are those of the number two or as a future chairman, then you may find your choice of remaining in the business will not close down opportunities for you but will give rise to opportunities of a different nature. It is highly likely that you already serve on another board as a Non-Executive Director. Possibly you are even a Deputy Chairman somewhere. Without question you can confidently aspire to be the Chairman of a significant business over time. The option of staying in the business will depend greatly upon the relationship you have already, or are able to forge, with the new Chief Executive who has been selected in your stead. Part of the Chief Executive's remit will be to ensure that he does not alienate those directors who have been unsuccessful in their bid to run the company. It is likely, therefore, that you will find a readiness to develop a strong collaborative partnership. What is equally likely is that the new Chief Executive will want to reorder the team in some way, thus giving you the opportunity to construct a role which can optimize your strengths and minimize his weaknesses. The Chief Operating Officer's role offers a useful model for some directors. Corporate life exists on the basis of a series of contracts. In this delicate situation you are effectively renegotiating the terms on which you give your allegiance both to the business and to the Chief Executive. If you are not already a Non-Executive this is the moment to be given permission to take one and possibly two Board seats. This should not be seen as a consolation prize. On the contrary, it is an opportunity to develop yourself and so maintain your dynamism such as to continue to give your best to your primary company.

The Non-Executive role

Boards can use the Non-Executive role as a means of assessing candidates for their own succession plan. It is a quite brilliant mechanism for allowing both sides to evaluate the other thereby removing some of the risk of tissue rejection on either side. I would not counsel any prospective Non-Executive Director to look at boards as guarantors of a Chief Executive position. In advising a Board on the appointment of the Chief Executive, however, a search firm would be likely to want to consider Board members themselves if only briefly and for purposes of elimination. It is uncommon for a Non-Executive to move into the role of Chief Executive but far from unknown (some of my own placements have subsequently gone on to be the Chief Executive). In considering a Non-Executive role it is worth considering the quality of the company, and your fit with the culture with considerable care. Even if you may never be the Chief Executive it is not improbable that you should become the Deputy Chairman and possibly even the Chairman in time. This is a route that seems particularly suited to senior Finance Directors, who may or may not have harboured ambitions to run a business but for whom the moment did not arise.

As you emerge from the selection process, beaten but unbowed, you should aim to enlist the services of those who have been engaged in this process with you:

- The Nominations Committee
- The search firm
- The successful candidate

The Board as a whole will need to ratify the decision for you to have one or more Non-Executive positions. As individuals, the Nominations Committee will have a strong sense of who you are. They will have seen you under pressure and will be privy to insights about you which are privileged. As Non-Executive Directors themselves they will be able to coach and guide you as you set about securing similar positions and, very possibly, put you in the way of specific opportunities. The search firm will be similarly situated but with access to many more Board situations and sufficient overview to properly assess your suitability for those Boards.

Looking outside

Your decision to stay with the organization, to accept perhaps the role as the number two or, at any rate, to renegotiate your position, will depend on your having come a fairly close second. You may need to face the harsh fact that there is a significant gap between your skill profile and that of the person who was selected. Perhaps you came third or fourth on the shortlist. There is no ignominy in this – to be third or fourth out of a significant cadre of managers is still a testimony to your talents. You will earn 60–70% of the income of the Chief Executive and spare yourself all the stress that goes with being number one. It may be the case, however, that the present company cannot accommodate your ambitions and continue to provide you with opportunities to learn. You need to try and understand what the issues have been and consider whether there is a deficiency amongst your skills that you can reasonably address and whether any coaching might be available to assist you. Then in all probability you will elect to look outside. If at this point you announce your intention to leave, then clearly you can enlist some support from those in or connected with the organization. If not, then you will need to call upon the relationships you have formed outside your present company.

This is where the long-standing contact with search firms can become important.

You may decide to look outside for other reasons. The most likely of these is that, having spent some months articulating your desire to be the Chief Executive of this company you know you cannot easily set aside the overall ambition, even if forced to surrender your hope of running your first choice business. How easily you can expect to make the transition to another enterprise as the Chief Executive will depend on your personal flexibility:

- Are you a one-company person or have you previously worked in other organizations?
- If you are a lifer in your particular business, have you had considerable depth and breadth of experience, serving on subsidiary Boards, operating overseas?
- Have you had exposure to other Boards, particularly as a Non-Executive?
- Do you have a profile outside your organization? Are you known in the financial community for example?
- Are you naturally someone who maintains good relationships with lawyers, consultants, search consultants? Do you therefore have a sense of the world beyond the company where you have spent your career?

If you have been a lifer in a major company and narrowly missed the top job there is little doubt that you will be shown opportunities and people will come to you even if you have studiously avoided the search community previously. To have narrowly missed out on the top job in so significant an enterprise is a mark of considerable expertise, talent and renown.

You may need to work hard to convince future Nominations Committees that you have sufficient flexibility to make the transition, but there is little doubt that you will have the opportunity to put your case. You will need to work harder if you have spent your entire career in a smaller company with limited experience of the outside world. Indeed, you may want to look closely at your motivation and reconsider.

Assuming, however, that you have answered in the affirmative to most of the above questions then yours will be an interesting quest in which, to a certain extent, you will be able to dictate terms. You may well find yourself, twenty-five or thirty years after first considering these questions, having to look very hard at the sort of organization you want to join. You may, of course, be prevented from joining a direct competitor owing to non-compete clauses in your contract so will need to think a little laterally to come up with the type of organization you would wish to join. It is probably advisable to be reasonably cautious and conservative in making your choice. If you have spent the entirety of your career in a large corporation with excellent support systems and structures you should probably stay in a large corporation which is similarly endowed. If all your experience has been of a domestic market it is unwise, at this juncture, to expand your horizons towards international ventures. You are now looking at entering the race to be a Chief Executive as an external candidate. For those hiring you the very fact that you are not from within represents a risk. It may useful to minimize that risk by offering the reassurance of knowledge. You might move sector but bring an understanding of similar distribution channels. The product focus may change but the consumer focus remain the same, by going say, from selling soap powder to selling bank accounts. Perhaps your particular expertise is in bringing together different cultures – look to find an environment which leverages, without necessarily replicating, that expertise; a post-merger situation, perhaps or – and this is risky – taking over from a founder.

Criteria for your search

It may be tempting to take the first interesting position that comes along. Better, however, to pause and make sure that all elements are in place to facilitate your success. These should include:

- Sufficient difference to provide challenge and to channel your natural thirst for knowledge.
- Sufficient similarities to give you a comfort zone.
- Sufficient similarities to give the Board, shareholders and stakeholders comfort.
- Sufficient logic that, when announced, your hire will resonate? Is the logic clear? Or will the market be baffled?

Your aim should be to achieve a rise in the share price when it is announced that you are the next Chief Executive. This, of course, sets high expectations for you but gives you a tremendous platform from which to meet them. Ultimately, the opportunities in the market will dictate the extent of your choice, but once confronted with some choice you need to look very closely at:

- The quality of the business over the last five or ten years. Refer closely to all available data especially brokers reports and back dated annual reports. Speak if possible to alumni, bankers, previous advisers try and calibrate the scale of the opportunity and its feasibility.

- Look very closely at the Board paying particular attention to the Chairman. Consider his personal track record. Is he someone from whom you can learn? Look at the quality of the hires he or she has made. Who do you know who has served with him on other boards, similarly the other Non Executives.

- Why has the business *not* yielded an internal candidate for Chief Executive? What are the implications in terms of the talent available in the organization as a whole?

- How long has the search been running? Has anyone turned the position down? Why?

- Consider the culture. What terms do people use to describe it? Are they ones with which you can identify. Is the culture one that has been successful in absorbing outsiders?

- Refer to your gut. Does this company excite and move you? Can you see yourself making a difference here? Does the organization inspire you to dream?

In short, measure the opportunity carefully against the risk. There should be elements of both in the proposition. While in the depths of despair having experienced the first and, so far, the only major disappointment of your career it may be hard to see that your failure merely frees you to be successful elsewhere. The process of learning about yourself, of reconsidering your options and of going through a further selection process, this time as an outside candidate, can enrich you and make of you a more attractive proposition than previously.

Looking for something else: the pluralist director

Perhaps you are in your fifties or late forties? You have had an absorbing and highly successful career but, having missed out on the top job, are disinclined to stay on until retirement, even in a Chief Operating Officer-style role with the opportunity for interesting Board positions. Your heart was with this company. You wanted to run it and, if you cannot, you do not want to stand by and watch others run it. Nor do you want to run something else. You have, however, abundant energy, enthusiasm, interests and skills. What is for you? Increasingly, the answer is a pluralist career. At its best this can be an intensely rewarding route, but much depends on your ability to structure an interesting portfolio and to deal with the ebbs and flows as situations change and opportunities come and go. There is no ideal portfolio but the following seems a good recipe for stimulation and achievement:

- One or two Non-Executive directorships
- One or two chairmanships
- One private equity opportunity or one international board
- One pro-bono, charitable or governmental role, subject to interest
- Start your own business or investment vehicle

The opportunities you take on should offer:

- Exposure to a large company. Having come from a large company, you will feel a degree of comfort in the environment. In general, large successful companies are able to recruit a broad array of successful Non-Executive Directors and to achieve some diversity in the boardroom. As you embark on a pluralist career you want to observe the masters and learn – the large company gives you scope to do so.

- Exposure to a small, possibly high-growth company, maybe one coming to the market. Here you will be dispensing some of your experience and acting as an elder statesman. You will continue to learn, however, principally about the speed of response required and the compromises that a smaller company can afford to make in the interests of growth.

- The opportunity to chair committees. The Board executes its responsibilities by means of committees, audit, remuneration and, increasingly, nominating. Indeed, committees are the expression of board authority. Chairing committees takes you into the very heart of issues in the business but also gives you additional experience of bringing people together to deliver decisions.

You may choose to start in a fairly modest way and then move onto higher-profile boards or move from Non-Executive to Chairman as you acclimatize yourself to the requirements. The challenge of a pluralist career is:

- To balance a number of different and competing interests
- To become familiar with the operating concerns of businesses outside your direct expertise
- To forge strong relationships with a broad range of executives
- To refine coaching and mentoring skills
- To protect the interests of shareholders by constant eval-

uation and re-evaluation of the conduct of the board and
the company at large

The lifestyle and role of a pluralist director will be very different from that of the Chief Executive you had previously
envisaged yourself being. Your concerns will be more diffuse
and you will feel less grounded. You will need to set yourself
up in an office (you may be given one with your premier role)
and with suitable support but you will be losing some of the
cut and thrust of life in an organization. You will also be losing
some of the onerous operational responsibilities but will be
replacing them with extraordinary responsibilities of over-
sight. This is not a life that suits everyone. Those who have a
strong desire to relate to an enterprise and to become synonymous with its identity will find an emotional vacuum in the
life of a pluralist director. The role better suits someone who is
intellectually interested in forms of governance, whose fascination with business extends to wanting to see different
businesses, facing separate challenges. It is a life for those who
are semi-detached, who are content with influence rather than
power. Occasionally the Non-Executives will markedly
change the course of a business by the deposition of an ineffec-
tive Chief Executive or Chairman. And of course, whenever
one of those two appointments is in the offing, it is the
Non-Executives who, to a certain extent, hold the fortunes of
the business in their hands. Once it was the case that a
Non-Executive directorship was a comfortable sinecure.
Those days are long gone. The Non-Executive plays a vital
supervisory role (hence the Supervisory Board), supporting
good decisions and preventing bad. The mark of a good board

is the breadth, involvement and independence of its Non-Executive team.

To be a pluralist director also requires someone with a subtle mind, who can spot potential conflicts of interest between organizations and ensure that at no time is he or she implicated. The Non-Executive team needs to show competence, but also needs to show unimpeachable integrity. The role further calls for someone whose fascination with business is such that they network actively around the commercial world, bringing new insights from different sources to refresh the board proceedings. There is also a self-serving element here. Your portfolio will be subject to change as you complete your term on one board or another board disappears in the wake of a major merger. You need to be kept informed of, and held in mind for, interesting opportunities which will be complementary. You can afford to take a risk from time to time – but you need to measure that risk, as ever, with care.

Looking for something else: business archangels

For those who want some of the variety of the pluralist career but also more operational exposure than can be had from a series of board meetings, there is an alternative: the business archangel – a term I have coined to describe a growing phenomenon is a relatively new notion. This is a variant on the notion of the business angel – the investor who provides start-up cash or significant financial support for a business but wants no other involvement. The concept of a business archangel has come about as a consequence of the generalized perception that a corporate career is not necessarily one that anyone would wish to pursue for life, coupled with the fact that there is (or certainly has been in recent years) abundant money available as risk capital from the growing group of individuals who have been made wealthy through their business career. After a successful career in business it may seem foolhardy to entrust money to novices. Better by far to put in the money but stick around to lend expertise too. Such a role can bring the variety of a pluralist career, the operational thrill that comes from seeing a new venture from inception or early stage through to profits and growth plus, and this is a significant factor, the chance to make money in the process. Indeed, a skilled business archangel can make far more by this route than by staying in the corporate fold.

Small and start-up businesses do not need board members who will maintain their distance and put in an appearance one day a month to review progress. They need more active support, more realistic appraisal of ideas, more careful reining in of enthusiastic excess and encouragement of ideas that have the look of certainty about them. The presence of a business archangel can be the salvation of a venture, since reasonable forms of governance can be established while the business is still in its infancy. This is not to suggest that bureaucracy and process are necessary or even desirable in a start-up – assuredly both are anathema. On the other hand, businesses frequently fall because of the inability of the founders and those with the initial idea to convert the idea into a workable commercial entity with the flexibility to grow and develop. The presence of someone with these corporate insights, who can prevent the founders becoming so obsessed with their own status, or brilliance that they become demonic, can be a critical factor in the overall success of the venture. The business archangel, then, does a range of the following:

- Provides first stage funding. Casts a very critical eye over the business plan and makes investment conditional upon the plan being watertight, thought through from every angle.

- Lends credibility in raising further funding, in any initial public offering, and in recruiting advisers, staff, customers and further investors.

- Chairs the business, providing coaching and mentoring to the entrepreneurial Chief Executive.

- Provides templates for how the business can be structured. Helps recruit to those templates.

- Reviews the business progress. Spots at an early stage any anomalies in the plan, any gap between plan and practice. Helps change the business model to one that is more successful.

- Helps the business raise its game – move into new markets, acquire more and higher calibre staff as the profits start to come in.

In short, a business archangel can unlock the potential of a brilliant idea and help convert it into a lasting commercial entity. There are of course numerous issues that you will need to balance, especially as you build a portfolio:

- How do you manage these investments tax effectively? There is no question but that you will need exceptional advice in this area.

- How do you identify the investments in the first place?

- How do you manage your exit route?

- How do you balance what time you give to which investments?

Some people make better business archangels than others. There is a very simple litmus test which will determine whether you have what it takes to engage with new enterprises. How comfortable are you in a small business? If you have grown up in a household where your parents were in the professions, then, after a good education, entered a blue-chip company, thereafter spending your career in large enterprises running major teams I would venture to suggest that when you touch down in a small business you will find yourself in alien territory. Small businesses conserve rather than spend money. They require corner-cutting, the rolling together of responsibilities, compromise on the quality of people brought into the business. They make much of a little, eschew routine and embrace ideas with vigour, putting them to the test and proving robust as some fail and others succeed. They require salesmanship far more than branding and marketing. They require close attention to the books far more than sophisticated deal doing. They require common sense rather than elaborate imaginative strategies. A new venture exists to put one product or service into the market place in the first instance. It needs to achieve that early success before it can proliferate. Certainly the business may need some services along the way but essentially it runs on as little as possible in order to establish the product or service. There is time later on for prettifying and it would be folly in a small business to try and build a brand before there is a product to attach to it. New small businesses require action, energy and very often a phlegmatic approach to perfection. Indeed, the mantra of a small business will be performance rather than perfection.

Companies move through, in anthropological terms, an interesting metamorphosis:

Corporate evolution: an anthropological model

Entrepreneurial venture	A handful of people explore a new idea	A working group – open and sharing

Leads to

A small business	The entrepreneurs open up the business to others who partake of and extend the idea.	A camp – a group of up to fifty people where everyone knows everyone else and where there is mutual respect and decisions are consensual. Leaders are the 'elders' those who came first, not necessarily those who are better in any way. Camps achieve actions by breaking down into small working groups.

Leads to

Medium and larger enterprises	The company expands and needs a fixed structure to enact its business. Roles and functions are enshrined in recognized norms. Rules are introduced.	A hierarchy. It is accepted that a hierarchy cannot function in a consensual fashion. A leader is appointed. He or she runs the hierarchy through clear strata in the venture and a process of command and control.

Most corporate people have become accustomed to the functioning of a hierarchy. Loosely speaking, all people have their place and assigned responsibilities. There are procedures and processes governing how things are done and a corporate precedent – a sense of the way things have habitually been done here. Hierarchies can accomplish much, but they do not tolerate blurred boundaries, shifting responsibilities and radical new perspectives on how things can be done. The truly corporate figure, whose natural home is a hierarchy, is better off as a business angel, making the investments but leaving others to realize them, than a business archangel. A business archangel can become a business demon if he or she seeks to impose the rules of the hierarchy on a camp-like environment.

Not all corporate people are wedded to a hierarchy. Indeed, the very best are highly flexible. When the best of corporate executives move to the boardroom, they move back into a camp environment, where a small group of equals meet to accomplish (or in this case agree) specific tasks, breaking down into working groups (committees) in order to so do. Led by a Chairman who is, essentially, first among equals, the Board is a very different entity from the company it oversees. A Chief Executive who has no board experience can be unsettled, indeed almost unseated, if he or she cannot adjust their style of operation to fit this different group. This insight from anthropology gives some credence to a unitary Board system that brings executives onto the board together with Non-Executives. It also lends support to the notion that budding Chief Executives should attain Board seats in other companies. While it is one thing to adapt to the way a Board operates it is no guarantee that someone who accommodates themselves to that move can make the move from large company to small. The Board, after all, supports a hierarchy and the comforting systems of that hierarchy remain below the Board and provide ballast. In an entrepreneurial venture there is no such backing.

The business archangel, then, is a route for someone who, for whatever reason, is at ease in a small company. In all probability, these will be people who grew up in a small business environment. Perhaps their parents were shopkeepers, hoteliers, ran small engineering companies or clothing factories. They may well have grown up steeped in the concerns of a small business, the need for creditors to pay promptly, the need to deliver on time, the requirement to raise additional funds, to keep the bank manager informed, to insure the premises, to provide cover for absent staff – the day-to-day minutiae which stand between success and failure. Another possibility may be that the partners of these would-be business archangels have always run small businesses. Others simply love business in all its forms; I have come across people in major businesses who are sleeping partners in entrepreneurial vehicles of their own, such is their fascination with commerce. If you want to make money from your investments and to be a success as a business archangel, then, above all, you need a very fundamental empathy with the concerns and objectives of a small operation. The subject is a big one and merits further detailed exploration, but I set it out here as one of the options available to you.

There might be one or two other options. You may choose to be a company doctor, although if this is your choice you will need to be a consumate operator, have considerable technical knowledge and be an enormous risk-taker (quite an unusual combination). It is a very particular person for whom such a life appeals and who, given that business can be a harsh and unforgiving world, can repeatedly resurrect themselves. Other options would seem to include interim management, but this is an option at the level below which we have been discussing and of doubtful use in this context. The greater need for interim support is at the functional level. The role of the Chief Executive requires continuity and continuum which, by its very nature, is absent in an interim solution. It would be a more logical choice for a company to put in a divisional director in a holding position or to, briefly, combine in one the roles of the Chairman and Chief Executive than to seek, from outside, someone on a limited contract. Perhaps, if you have some of the attributes of the business archangel but are too hands-on to want to advise, you can set up on your own. This is likely to be an option for you if you are in your late thirties or your forties. I can think of few entrepreneurs who have struck out alone in their fifties. Given the panoply of talents you have, the next phase of your career can be as rewarding (in all senses of the word) as the last phase, albeit a little different from that which you had planned.

One of the sad truths that I have been obliged to acknowledge over many years in search is that there is a limited supply of talent and more interesting situations than there are talented people to take them up. If you have reached the point of being considered for a prestigious role at the head of a business, there is little question that you have some very considerable talents. You may have failed to secure the job that you passionately wanted, but this does not mean that you will be any less successful in the long-term. You have, perhaps, lost a game, or even a set, but not the match. Every year top seeded players surprise us by falling out in the early stages of major tennis tournaments. These are mere setbacks and, invariably, the top seed recovers himself, finds his form and, adamant that he will not allow a second setback, throws himself into the rest of the season with renewed determination. In all probability, he will come through on top. Indeed, the experience has hardened his resolve and made success the more likely. The crushing disappointment of coming second or third will before long give way to a sense of opportunity. Your pioneering zeal will assert itself, together with you sense of invincibility and you will take charge, possibly even for the very first time, of your own destiny. Success may have eluded you once, but remains tantalizingly within reach . . .

Afterword

t seems inappropriate to give the last word to the runner-up in the race to be Chief Executive. What of the victor? After all your years of preparation, numerous successes and now the acknowledgement of your talents, what happens next? Once the elation passes, comes the reality that, like so much else, Chief Executive status, though hard won, is easily lost. What will ensure that having made it to the top you stay there? The short (and predictable) answer to this is that there is no short answer. If there were we would probably not have become so accustomed to corporate failure led by unsuccessful Chief Executives. In these closing words I want to look a little at the elements which, together, might enable you to achieve sustained success.

Your first enemy is complacency. In soccer one of the best moments to score a goal is when the other side are celebrating having just scored themselves. In your jubilation at having secured the top job do not be caught off-guard. Look instead to score easy successes, to accustom people to the fact that you are innately successful. If you can establish this perception through relatively simple strikes you give yourself time to accomplish the bigger, complex successes. Dealing sensibly with the others who were on the shortlist alongside you may be an immediate way of gaining the approval of the Board and of other observers. In the previous chapter I have outlined the benefits of being a number two and becoming, perhaps, the Chief Operating Officer or Group Managing Director. Could the runner up to you fulfil this function? This may not be a workable solution, should it not be judicious treatment of your talented peers, all the same, will be an important signal.

While you should manage the relationships down through the business there is an enormously important relationship to forge above you, namely that with the Chairman. It is a certainty that the Chairman has been your strong advocate. No Board would appoint a Chief Executive who could not command the support of the Chairman. In all likelihood you and he have already established a rapport, you see things similarly, you speak the same language and dream similar dreams. You will have expressed a vision for the business that chimed with his, will have struck a chord as the man to make his vision live. It is even possible that the present Chairman is a previous boss and mentor of yours, if the Chairman comes from within. Perhaps you are re-creating a former partnership. Whatever the context, now that you are established in the role of Chief Executive you need to start over again, to go back to first principles in agreeing how the two of you will work together. How did the Chairman work with the previous Chief Executive? What worked? What didn't? And do not focus exclusively on the Chairman but, guided by the Chairman, work your way around the Non-Executives. Around the Board there are many years of accumulated wisdom that you can use to work in your favour. You will need to extend this process of relationship building beyond the boardroom with key advisers, customers and important contacts who influence the course of the enterprise. The early weeks and months are ones when you are establishing your credentials and, at the same time, seeing the business through the eyes and ears of a broad range of interested parties. You are learning to soak in and ingest information, to sift through it and take the richest parts to form a part of your own strategy and approach. But while doing this you must also act. Act to ensure that profits grow, that margins or productivity improves.

Much of your ability to succeed will depend upon your energy. In previous jobs you have worked very hard. In some ways you will have worked harder then than now, ploughing through paper and problems and seemingly never reaching the end of the tasks assigned to you. As Chief Executive the balance will shift and you will delegate much of the routine. But you will find yourself working harder than ever before. The burden of accountability falls to you; you are on duty twenty-four hours a day. How you conduct yourself will inform the perception of the company. A word of irritation to a shareholder at the Annual General Meeting in front of a journalist can be harmful, giving good copy for the newspapers and bad press for the company. This may be a trivial example but it is important to be on your guard or on duty at all times. It will take time to acclimatize to the extent to which you are in the public eye. In an earlier book I wrote extensively about the shadowy nature of our business leaders. This is changing. Business issues have unquestionably acquired new prominence in the reporting of news. With the fall of communism and the move of most on the left towards the centre across much of Europe there is a far greater recognition that the capitalist model is one that concerns us all and is more robust than other systems. As resistance has fallen, interest has grown. There is greater recognition that business matters and that Chief Executives have power. They used to be better able to blend into the background. Now they cannot assume their anonymity. They cannot relax their guard. It takes extraordinary stamina to tolerate a life in which you cannot relax. The driven and energetic have the edge on those of us who are more laid back – they seldom relax and so can deal with the requirement to represent the business round the clock.

Very often Chief Executives will be called upon to represent the business in a social setting and there is an enormous social element to the role. Many relationships are cemented in an informal environment, in the guise of a pleasant cultural or sporting event, at which all parties will be accompanied by their partners. Indeed, the views of partners can become very influential and it is important to charm and win over all those around you, not simply the immediate person you need to influence. Your celebrity within the company will require you to attend numerous ceremonies around the globe, assuming that this is an international business. Your diary will fill up from first thing in the morning until last thing at night, and seldom will you have time that you can genuinely call your own. Even your marriage will become part of this project (if it wasn't already) and you will, at times, lose sight of your private persona so permanent will be the public one become. This calls for tremendous stamina, tolerance and self-containment. If you have vast reserves of energy, if for example you need relatively little sleep, you will have an advantage over those with more dormouse-like tendencies. Similarly, if you have tremendous powers of concentration. If you are the sort of

person who can make use of stray moments, caught in an air-
port lounge, in a taxi, waiting for a meeting, to refresh yourself
with something that you enjoy, then you will manage to keep
hold of some kind of perspective, a sense of proportion.

This sense of proportion is all important. It amounts to judgement. Some people will fail – you have seen people fail from
lack of judgement on your way to where you are currently –
simply because they start to believe their own myth. They
become alarmingly solipsistic and are the centre of their own
world. They come to believe that they are Chief Executive as if
by divine right and that they are invincible. They lapse into
complacency, failure and disillusion and, if they cannot be
stopped in time, take their company with them. Your success
will depend greatly upon your ability to read situations, to
analyse them accurately and to form the right judgements.
You will know when to buy a business or when to retreat,
when to promote someone and which are the right jobs to
develop particular people with particular skills. You will
know who to trust and who to be cautious of, whose judgement is reliable and whose faulty. Most of all, you will know
your own impulses and you will hold yourself in check. You
will continue to listen, you will accord credit where it is due
and take only that which is legitimately yours – if, indeed, you
need that much. This quality of judgement is imprecise;
people either have it or they do not. It is easily undermined.
Several errors of judgement and you are likely to be removed
from office.

While you need to be mentally and morally robust you need
also to be physically robust. Your good health and well being

are extraordinary factors in your success. You will be putting your body under tremendous strain. You will be forced to eat many meals of a rich and ultimately unhealthy variety, to sit long hours in cramped planes and to spend equally long hours in stuffy offices. Your opportunities for exercise will be limited. You need to be in outstanding physical condition before you launch your career as a Chief Executive and, however limited your time, find some to give attention to your health. A period of prolonged ill health could be extremely problematic both for you personally and for the organization (I have already noted the impossibility of appointing an interim Chief Executive). If your health starts to show signs of strain then confidence in you will start to falter. We invest our leaders with all manner of superhuman capabilities, not least of which is rosy good health and you run the risk of losing a little of your leader's mystique – of being somehow stronger in all respects than the rest of us – if your health suffers.

Your ultimate success, however, will depend upon two things beyond your control. In the first place it will depend upon your personality and the way in which you unite that personality with those around you. Having studied skills and attributes of Chief Executives I am forced to conclude, in the end, that force of character, strength of personality, an ease, confidence, self-assurance, counts for more than any text book skills, being the fount from which trust and respect will flow. Your ability to form and sustain relationships. Your ability to bring people round to your way of thinking, to rally people, give them confidence, sustain them through difficult periods. All of these skills are to do with personality, an accident of birth.

Second, you require your moment, your *Zeitgeist*, the intervention of serendipity. You have led a charmed life so far (notwithstanding some of the early agonies which have given you this drive for success) but securing your place in the business history books will depend upon some unpredictable momentary event which you, the ever watchful Chief Executive, can grasp and make your own. Spotting a major merger, recognizing a kindred spirit and appointing them to work alongside you, exploiting a contemporary need for whatever your business can supply in a new market at the right time. The permutations are endless. Alexander Fleming might never have discovered penicillin but for a fortuitous accident and his felicitous recognition of the implications of that accident. But for the fact that the First World War was fought in trenches, where there was room for little else but contemplation, we would not have had the outpouring of poetry, not seen in any war before or since. Had Anne Boleyn borne Henry VIII a healthy son Britain would never have had the Reformation, and very possibly not the Civil War or even the Industrial Revolution. Accidents of history; events beyond our control shape us and our environment. The best that we can hope for is that, when our moment comes, we catch it, recognize it and act on it. Again and again, Thomas Hardy expresses this fleeting moment in which fate or chance offers up opportunity for us to take or ignore:

> *Faintheart in a Railway Carriage*
> At nine in the morning there passed a church,
> At ten there passed me by the sea,
> At twelve a town of smoke and smirch,
> At two a forest of oak and birch,

And then, on a platform, she:
A radiant stranger, who saw not me.
I said, 'Get out to her do I dare?'
But I kept my seat in my search for a plea,
And the wheels moved on. O could it but be
That I had alighted there.

You may never have this moment. You may not sit next to the right person on the plane, or take the right call or see the brilliant maverick in your midst. This does not mean that you will fail, but it might mean that your success is of a fairly ordinary and limited kind, minding the status quo, being neither very wrong nor very right. If, however, you do have such a moment, if you find the Amoco to go with your BP, or the ASEA to go with your Brown Boveri, then, assuming you can make it work, success might just be within your grasp. You will achieve not just corporate mastery but something close to corporate wizardry. Many will try and explain how you have mastered the art of success and might come close to understanding the forces of circumstance and of personality that have come together in your being. All they will have succeeded in doing, however, is to have understood your particular success. They will not have uncovered a formula that we can replicate whenever we want to succeed. In this book I have brought together the sum of my observations over twenty years or more of how people make it to Chief Executive. That is as much as it is possible to do, the discovery of the elixir of success I must leave to a better alchemist than I.

Index